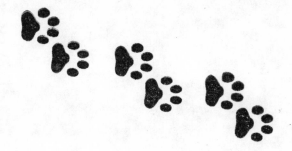

TWO LABS AND A BLOODHOUND

The Adventures Begin

Kipper, Tracker and Beau

By Judy Greenawalt

authorHOUSE®

AuthorHouse™
1663 Liberty Drive, Suite 200
Bloomington, IN 47403
www.authorhouse.com
Phone: 1-800-839-8640

First published by AuthorHouse 1/12/2010

ISBN: 978-1-4490-5215-7 (e)
ISBN: 978-1-4490-5213-3 (sc)
ISBN: 978-1-4490-5214-0 (hc)

Library of Congress Control Number: 2009913108

Printed in the United States of America
Bloomington, Indiana

This book is printed on acid-free paper.

DEDICATION

This is for you Irene, the dear friend you are and co-conspirator in the loving of animals. Thanks for your encouragement to do this.

Irene Mc Harg and eight week old Tracker

*Sunkist, Patches, Harley, and Socrates
discover it's not good to eat the yellow snow.*

CONTENTS

ACKNOWLEDGEMENT

The happenings and adventures you are about to read about are all true as can be verified from the people who in our life have witnessed them, and/or have been victim of some of the happenings.

In the Bible there is scripture where God gave dominance to Adam and Eve and their offspring over all the creatures of the land. Somehow there are certain critters who either did not get the message passed down to them through the ages, or think that it either does not pertain to them, or they have just decided to ignore us humans for the most part. I swear to God some of these critters have been a "plant" by the Master Himself to test us our strength and to see who can outwit whom and yet remain in control. Sometimes it was the dog, cat, or ferret that won, and sometimes it was not exactly a Kodak moment that was witnessed or experienced!

Many thanks to the people who provided us with these wonderful pets, for our life would have been void of the unconditional love and companionship these animals have provided throughout the years.

Many thanks to Chris for the wonderful birthday gift of Socrates; this Yellow Lab was so loyal, smart, funny, and a great companion. You know he was dearly loved. All those puppies sure gave Bita and Snickers a daily run for the money.

Many heartfelt thanks to the breeder who provided me with Misty, and to Jack who gave us one of Misty's sister's pups, who was named Clyde. These wonderful Dobermans provided us a lot of memories, love, protection, and companionship for many years. People around us also discovered the gentle and wonderful nature of this wonderful and too often misunderstood breed.

Thanks to Mr. Asa Elwell for Sporty Beagle IV. A greater hunting dog there never was. Of course he would take off on a scent and you might not see him again for a bit, but he always came home, nevertheless. Most of the time it would be under his own steam, but many times human intervention would have a hand in it when he wandered too far, and was found resting by someone who would read his tags and call us with his whereabouts. We would go and retrieve him with no questions asked, happy to have him safe and alive and home with us again. Of course he was always very happy to see us and would gladly stay home until the next time he got on a track and his nose overtook his common sense. Such was meant to be the life of a hound!

Many thanks Don Wyman for locating Beauregard for us. Marley would have had some real competition with Beau had they been raised together. I really think Beau is the quieter of the two, but not by much I can assure you! Beau is truly the best bad dog we ever had.

Many thanks Wanda who gave me Kipper. It was the most wonderful gift of love given freely and from the heart. I know it was one of the hardest things she ever had to do. Remember while reading through the text Kipper is the good one!

Many thanks Shannon Pruden for Patches. Little did we know when Patches came into our lives there would be a special place he would steal and stay there forever in my heart.

Many thanks Rachel Doane for Harley Davidson Dawg, our very first Labrador Retriever. He came to us when Toby, my husband was very ill and Harley's daily companionship and antics helped us all through the post-op recovery. I knew he was a very good boy when he chewed up that antique chair and he did me a favor, as I never really did care for the chair anyway.

Many thanks Rick Jones for Sunkist. He was the biggest, most loveable, very intelligent dog anyone could hope for. It seemed like he could read your mind most of the time. He was another wonderful surprise Christmas gift I will never forget.

Many thanks Joe and Joyce Engle for raising great family-oriented dogs, and for allowing us to bring Colonel Tracker into our home. He was a dream I had for many years that I thought would never come true. This Bloodhound baby has brought much happiness to our household and adventures none of us would have ever experienced before.

Many, many thanks to Barbara Sargent for always being available to pet sit, watch over, care for, and love our animals as we do when we had to be away. They all love you as much as they love us. And no, you still cannot dog nap Beau in spite how much he always wants to go with you.

Many thanks to Dr. Lanfair, our first Veterinarian when we were kids and through our early adulthood. This wonderful man was always available day or night, seven days a week, and the door was always opened. No matter how tired or how busy he was, he always greeted everyone with a big smile. This is one wonderful perk of living in a small town and having a vet for your neighbor.

Many, many thanks to Greylock Animal Hospital and the entire staff of wonderful veterinarians and techs who have always been there for our animals and their care. All of your concerns, compassion, and advice have been greatly appreciated all through the years.

Many thanks to my husband for all the great planned and unplanned dogs and other critters you have brought home that have brought us much happiness as well as heartache when they passed on. Sunkist and Tracker were wonderful surprises and Christmas presents we shared for many years. I am sure we will be reunited with them all someday when we too cross over that <u>RAINBOW BRIDGE</u>.

So, for all of our dogs we had as kids, for all the ones in our married life: the Sporty Beagles I.II.III, and IV, Christy, Colonel Klink, Misty, Clyde, Harley, Patches, The Red Dog, Sunkist, Socrates, Kipper, Beauregard, and the Tracker Dude, and some we may have forgotten, I say thank you for making our lives a lot richer by being our pets. Thank you to our heavenly Father for creating all of them, and to all the people whose names I have also forgotten who have provided us with these puppies and other critters.

Many thanks to Elaine Clark for having the patience of a saint while editing and offering advice. A greater friend everyone should have. She whips up a pretty good beef stew too.

Now sit back, grab a cup of tea or whatever and relax. I hope the words you are about to read will make you laugh and cry, while you are able to picture in your mind what we have experienced, because it really has been an adventure! Every day is an adventure when your dog owns you, because they all live for the moment. You never know what they are going to do next!

Beauregard, Tracker, & Kipper

CHAPTER ONE
The Adventure Begins

Ever since I can remember I have loved dogs and all kinds of animals, but horses and dogs have always been my favorite. My mother was not a cat lover, so as kids we did not have a true residential cat living with us, and that is not a bad thing. Since I have been married we have always had a cat, or two, or three, or four, and mostly always a dog or two or five. There have been times when there wasn't a dog in our home, but not for long.

As a child, my husband tells me he always had hunting dogs, all named Sport and mostly beagles, and they were used for hunting, and were never inside dogs like ours of today are.

My first dog as a child was a German Shepard named Rex that my grandfather gave to me. I was the only child at the time. But as we all know, the years go by in what seems a blink of an eye and you forget all the details about how your pets leave your life. In spite of the years that have passed and as young as I was when he was taken away from me, I have never forgotten Rex and the companionship and love we shared. I never knew how or who took him from my life, yet I still have my suspicions how Rex disappeared, as he was there one day and gone the next day when I woke up. I have never forgotten that experience of loosing a pet, nor have I forgotten why no one would ever tell me what happened to Rex. Even though I have never been able to confirm the facts, I still have my suspicions of what happened.

Time went by, and two sisters came into my life. When we became older, one day out of the blue mom brought us home a beagle puppy we named Buttons. Maybe my begging for a dog all those years had something to do with it? Unfortunately, two years later he disappeared like Rex did too, and being older I can remember voicing my opinion about pets that suddenly disappeared without a trace. The disappearance of Buttons was like a knife into my heart and brought up memories from long ago that I thought were buried.

Then there was Butch the Beagle followed by Duke a black Lab mix. Then along came Blackie, a black Cocker Spaniel who clearly loved my sister Patricia the best of any of us. Next was Fudge, a beagle that lived with us until I got married and left the nest. Because my husband had a series of Beagles growing up all named Sport, our last Beagle became Sport Beagle IV. So you can see that we have had dogs weaving in and out of our lives in a timeframe that seems like forever.

Since we have been married we have had dogs, mostly hunting dogs that really never had to hunt. There was sporty the Beagle IV, Annie the Beagle and her pup; I have forgotten his name. Next we had Damien Beagle, two German Shepards named Christie and Colonel Klink. A Shepard named Killer who was the sweetest, gentlest, smartest dog you ever saw. He acquired the name Killer because of his beautiful color and sweet laid back disposition; a dumb name or what for such a sweet dog? He could never hurt a fly. We will never forget our two Dobermans Misty, Clyde, a few Yellow Labs named Harley Davidson Dawg, Sunkist Golden Boy, Sawed Off Socrates, and General Beauregard. One Chocolate Lab Kipper and a Bloodhound named Colonel Tracker Hound Dawg. Kipper, Beau, and Tracker are our current resident "dog kids" now, and probably will be our last as we are getting along in years. But, we love them all dearly as they do us, as you will see by the affection and the antics they shower us with.

As I sit here on the couch with laptop in my lap, hunting and pecking the letters and numbers out, I am slightly distracted by the surrounding events passing me by one simply cannot ignore. Kipper or "The Chocolate Child" as he is sometimes called, has claimed the doggy bed for a well-deserved nap. He is obviously running or chasing a rabbit or a ball in his sleep; his dark brown doggy legs move every now and then as does his tail wag ever so slightly while making a half-hearted woof sounds in his sleep. He is such an elegant looking Chocolate Lab for a six-year-old dog. He is the perfect dog most of the time, and he is called "the good one" because he really is the best-behaved dog by human standards. His dark brown silky fur is as dark as a piece of semi-sweet chocolate that seems faded during day light, and is often taken for a black Lab because of the deep, dark chocolate color he is.

Beauregard, the Yellow Lab has claimed the blue recliner with the doggy dad scent and his upside stature, (lying upside down) is the perfect position for camouflaging the almost lethal flatulence he expels today while he dreams away. I hope he is dreaming and not plotting something to pull on us! He is laying upside down on his back while his long legs hang over the edge of the arm of the chair for a reason; he likes to. What better way to squeeze out those silent-but-deadly doggy farts in hopes the others might get the blame. He has acquired the nicknames of "Blonde Baby" and sometime "The Golden Child", but he isn't so sweet at the moment. He raises and lowers his tail slowly as he sleeps, allowing a silent-but-deadly aroma into the room air, and I now know for sure which dog stole my other half of the toasted raisin and cream cheese bagel from the counter this morning. Counter surfing by the dogs is not allowed in our house. The dogs have been trained not to touch anything on the counters, table, or sink, but every now and then, and it is a rare moment, a piece of toast or bagel takes a disappearing act. I half-heartedly expect the living room wallpaper to come peeling down at any moment as it is in the middle of January and 11 below zero outside, and I cannot open any windows. I suddenly realize now why Trouble, Samantha, and Runte, our three cats have taken refuge napping on the couch in the adjacent living room with their paws covering their faces as they nap. And some folks think they lay on that couch to soak up the sun streaming in from the bay window. I look around the room and half chuckle to myself thinking what non-animal owners are missing in their lifetimes. Yep, there is definitely going to be more yellow fur deposited in the nooks and crannies of that chair when Beau arises. Great contrast with the brown and red furs from the other two dogs that could be hidden in the corners of the stuffing. Might even be some grey, white, and black furry deposits down deep when the cats get their turns to the chair, dogs allowing this of course.

Tracker the Bloodhound is curled up next to me with his coppery head full of wrinkles and his long ears flopped across my arms. His head weighs heavy on my arm, but it is most comforting as he snuggles and snores in rhythmic song, and Bloodhounds really can snore. I casually glance over at him and ponder when did that nose got so big? I swear it is always working! Even as he naps you can see the black edges moving and twitching with each inspiration and expiration of air he breathes. His silky cooper fur has lost all traces of the black he had blended with the red fur when he was born, and his coppery coat has taken on a soft curl going down his back whiles he is silently growing each day and slipping out of his puppy hood state. And I have noticed that his white spot on his chest that resembles a clover is as white as a new fallen snow has not changed shape, but has grown as he has grown. His long legs are gracefully tucked under his long body as he rests. He has rightfully acquired the nickname of "The Dude" along with "The Carmel Kid." Such is the life of theses great hunters who have never had to work a day in their lives, and probably never will.

They are all so peaceful and quiet now, giving off the "good dog" picture that dog owners all desperately would like to boast of pets they own. Half an hour ago they were busy playing and strewing their doggy toys about like kids as they were taking them out of their toy basket. Strange how they never pick up their toys when they are bored and finished with the ones they have dragged and strewn all over our home. I really need to try and train them to put their toys back in their basket when they are through with them. Like that might really happen! They really are so entertaining and fun when they are playing like this. Anybody that has owned any animal will tell you there is no such thing as the perfect pets all of the time. Every living critter, be it animal or human, starts out as a baby and is nurtured somehow by someone who is in an older form of life than their own. It distress me when I hear people complain about a young child or pet that has done something wrong or done some mischievous thing, and we all have done this as humans. We often forget the young are just that, young that need guidance, love, and understanding by someone older than they. Patience can be worn to a frazzle, and it can be frustrating when you are trying to teach someone or something like an animal and they cannot speak back. Yet, as you really get to know a child or an animal, and if you really watch them and are paying attention to them, they are in essence talking to you in their own way. Not so much in words, but with body movements. Human babies and animal babies are really not that much different from each other. The only exception is animals do not need to be dressed in clothes while human babies need to be dressed and diapered. For a dog it is look in their eyes, a wag of their tails, that wet, slobbery, soft tongue that tells you they love us. Tracker will even stand on his hind legs, wrap his paws around your neck while looking down at you, while wagging his tail when you least expect it. Because of his large size of 120 plus pounds of puppy, this totally freaks out some people when they see this dog do this. He is so gentle when he does this, and I know he is saying, "I love you" in his own way. I must admit it must look weird, but he is a dog and since he cannot speak with words, he speaks with his actions. And after owning a Bloodhound I thoroughly and completely understand why criminals being tracked down by these very large, bright, and elegant creatures will surrender once the Bloodhound tracks them down. It must be all that the drool!

Beau and Kipper like most Labs are very loveable, and I think the breed has been misnamed. Although the Labrador has an elegant name and was meant to help the fisherman, and has down the ages become one of the most perfect pets, maybe they should have been named Lapadores because of they way they love to sit in your lap, and will race you to the couch or bed for the best seat in the house. No chance of the couch or recliner staying empty for long in our house if you happen to get up out of it for something; one of the dogs will hop right in completely guilt-free like it is expected of them to do so. And oh the dirty looks you get from them when you command them to surrender the place they have stolen and want to call their own.

I love all breeds of dogs, but while I tend to like the larger dog breeds, my sisters tend to go for the smaller breeds. I love working with the large breeds because of their size, companionship, and ability to learn commands. That's my excuse and I am sticking to it.

On the next few pages I will share some adventures and stories of our beloved pets. All stories are true, and you had to have been here to appreciate the dogs. How they interacted with the other critters is so amazing, and it is also sad that animals of different species can get along, while there are some humans who cannot. Perhaps all of us humans need to look at the animal world a little more intensely as we all could learn something, and then bit by bit maybe the entire world would surely be a better place.

The story will basically start off with one of my German Shepards mainly because she had a very unique way of driving us nuts. I swear to God that dog would sit and plot how to get even with us when we left the house or even if she suspected we were in the process of leaving and we did not take her with us.

Judy and Christy

CHAPTER TWO
Christy of Windcrest

Christy was one of the cutest and friendliest puppies of the "C" litter I had ever seen. I had been going to dog obedience school and training another dog I had when the instructor approached me and told me they had a new litter, and I was welcomed to come and see the three-week-old pups. We talked it over at home and decided we would just look, as we did not need another dog at this point. However, things happened and decisions got changed along the way. A friend of mine had recently lost her husband to cancer and was really having a very tough time of it. The six-month-old Shepard-mix pup I had been training sensed that she was going through a tough time and bonded with her as he did with us. One could see that she was so much at peace and her eyes seemed so much brighter when she was with this dog, as were her kids. I thought long and hard about how much we loved this dog and all the work I had put into the training of him, but I could see a longing in the eyes of the pup's eyes too whenever my friend left our house. He was a good puppy. He loved us, was loyal, smart, completely house broken, yet something in my gut was telling me he needed to be with her and her family more. I talked it over with my husband and we agreed maybe it was meant to be that the puppy should be with her, and we could get another puppy somewhere down the line of time.

I called her two days later, and within fifteen minutes the whole gang arrived to collect him. My heart was broken, but deep inside I knew it was the right thing to do. That pup brought them twelve years of happiness and unconditional love in a time of their lives when they needed it the most. My friend said he was the best dog she ever owned. Did I see him? Yes. And he still showed the love and affection to me that I showered on him.

Like I said earlier, when I saw the litter of pups, I did not have any intentions of buying one right away, but the black and silver female, the runt, kept coming over, crawling in my lap, chewing on my fingers one minute while giving me puppy kisses the next. I don't know what came over me, but two weeks later I put a deposit on her and at eight weeks old I took her home. I decided her registered name was going to be Christy of Windcrest after The WindCrest Kennels from whence she came, but I would call her Christy. She also became the puppy from hell the minute I put her in the car and headed for home! She had not been the car for 5 minutes when she decided to take a poop without warning on the floor mat on the passenger side of the car. I pulled over, not alarmed, as a pup is a baby and she was in an entirely new environment. I quickly scooped up the poop and tossed it, and she settled down as we headed for home.

It did not take her long to sniff out the place she was to call home and literally take right over. The cat kept outrunning her and was planning a permanent game of hiding without the seeking when Christy decided the cat made a wonderful chew toy. To hell with the toys she had, this thing moved and moved fast, and it made noises too; it fought back and Christy thought this was fun. The cat thought otherwise and made me well aware of her thoughts as she hissed loudly at me as she went tearing by, running up the stairs to escape. Christy could not get up the stairs due to a thing called, Mr. Gate. Mr. Gate blocked the stairway that kept a busy little boy and puppy safe from going upstairs unsupervised. Little did we know Christy would soon learn how to open Mr. Gate, go up stairs, and search and destroy! And destroy she did!! Nothing was safe. Shoes were wonderful, socks were yummy especially when one chewed out the toes, bedding and pillows came off the already made beds so slick, and pillows were wonderful things to shred with those shark-like puppy teeth. What a mess I had to clean when she discovered she could open the gate.

When we were not home I tried to keep her in my kitchen, gated off in a warm and cozy corner with food, water, doggy bed and toys as we did our other pups, and this worked well until she hit the five-month-old mark. It was like a bell had gone off in her little head and the real mischief began. We also had an eighteen-month-old toddler who loved the puppy and he was so amazed with the mess when I opened the door the first time we found the attack of Christy. I was not amazed as I was pregnant, tired from working all day, and was not at all impressed by the mess and destruction I saw. How could a puppy this young be so smart and yet such a devil when left alone? Curtains were pulled down. A whole box of laundry detergent was torn open and strewn all over the kitchen. There was a trail of toilet paper from the bathroom going into the kitchen, through the living room along with what was left of the roll of paper towels that was found hiding under the dining room table. It was a miracle this dog didn't get hurt or die as she punctured a can of shaving cream that was all over the bathroom floor, and the final straw was that she literally tore the toilet seat off of the toilet. How she ever managed get to these things we will never know.

I knew my husband would never in his wildest dreams believe the mess I had found unless he saw it for himself. So, I did what any irritated spouse would do; I left it for him to see, gathered up my toddler and headed for our local pet shop to purchase a crate. Mistake number two!

When Toby saw the mess he could not believe it either, that a puppy could do so much destruction in such a short period of time as she had always been so good when left alone before. We picked up the mess not even saying a word to each other and restored the house to order while the darling puppy looking innocent played quietly with our son. But after this mess she made, I just knew she wasn't as innocent and sweet as she was presenting herself at this moment. While TJ was laughing and playing, I just knew Christy was plotting and scheming for her next day of fun and adventures while we both were at work, but so was I.

While I was fixing supper, Toby opened the crate package I had purchased earlier and was putting it together. The puppy and the baby watched with interested while Toby was reading directions trying how to figure out how to put the crate together. TJ chattered away non-stop and thought it was a new play thing. He was too little to understand that this was a cage meant to keep the house safe and the puppy confined safely while we were away for short periods of time. All the while this was going on at our house, little did I know that a physician I worked with was basically going through the same thing with a male pup he bought from the same litter.

It seems his wife had gone out for the afternoon and she put the puppy in her laundry room as she always did, and seeing how he shared the same DNA as Christy, all hell let loose in their house too the minute she closed the door and left. They must have telepathically communicated, because the chaos that I heard about was nothing at our house compared to what happened at theirs.

They had table legs chewed beyond recognition. Chair cushions were completely unrecognizable, but resembled rags that had been shredded up and strewn all over. Lamps with no cords, magazines that looked like someone had thrown confetti all over the house, and her supper was a memory. That's right; after all the mess he created, that dog even devoured the roast she had prepared, but not yet cooked for supper. At first when she walked in the front door she thought their house had been vandalized until she saw a sleeping puppy under a thing that used to be a chair, but resembled something indescribable. She did not know whether to cry or sigh with relief when she discovered what had happened, but she was really upset when she discovered the supper she had planned was gone. I did not feel so bad after I heard that account because it got worse.

Shirley called her husband at the office, told him what had happened and he could not believe what she was describing. She informed him he was going to believe it, because the evidence was going to wait for him to see it first hand when he got home, and he better stop and get a pizza on the way home from the office, or it was peanut butter and jelly for supper. Bill told me that when he opened that door he nearly dropped as he surveyed the mess. He agreed he would help her clean the mess, and he had forgotten on purpose not to pick up a pizza as he did not believe things were as bad as she stated. He decided he would graciously call in a pizza order, go get it and pick up a crate on the way home. His wife told him to take the dog with him too as she was in no mood to spend even ten minutes alone with the puppy right now. He graciously agreed to take the puppy with him when she reminded him he was the one who had brought the dog home for himself after the last child has left their nest. Things just got worse on his mission!

The puppy seemed really happy to go for what he thought was just a ride in the car. Bill stopped at the same pet store I did earlier and bought the same kind of crate, ran next door and picked up the pizza. Time frame for the dog to be alone in the car unattended was about twenty minutes. He put the crate and the pizza in the trunk of his a 1969 Firebird convertible for what he thought was safekeeping. When he opened that car door he said he nearly crapped his pants. He could not believe a puppy left alone in the car for twenty minutes could do so much. His passenger seat was chewed so the wire frame was showing through where the upholstery should be. The knob of the stick shift was completely chewed off, and the rear view mirror was lying on the floor in a heap. Two seatbelts were fragmented from chewing so that all remained were buckles. He said he was in such a state of shock he said nothing, started the car, found a screwdriver and placed it in the shaft of the stick shift so he could shift the car, and headed home. When he pulled into the driveway, his wife greeted him, looked over the mess in the car from the dog, took the pizza and said "good dog" as they went into the house. To make a long story short, the crate plan did not work for them either! Just to maintain their sanity, they ended up hiring a permanent dog sitter for that dog every time they left the house.

I didn't have to work for the next two days, so I knew this would be a good time to orient Christy to the crate. I started out with short periods of time not realizing all the time the dog was scoping it out and plotting. I knew she was very intelligent, just how intelligent she was we were about to find out. The first day back to work was an experiment and plan that literally backfired on us because of the intelligence of a dog we underestimated.

Toby's parents lived nearby so his mother offered to check on the dog a couple of times a day to make sure she was adjusting okay to her new situation. When I got home that night I wanted to cry. Much to my dismay, our crate investment and plan was not such the great disabler for Christy's search and destroy missions as I thought it would be. When I opened the front door of the house, to my surprise I found yet another terrible mess. There was that darn Christy in the middle of the living room in the crate with the bottom of the crate kicked out and the living room in shambles. The TV was knocked over, as was the lamp. Plants were on the floor. The coffee table was upside down. The couch was out of place. And there sat my beautiful puppy just a wagging her tail and happy as a clam to see me like nothing had happened. The crate had a slide in bottom, and it looked secure when put together. The designer obviously never had a dog that thought like a prisoner looking for an escape route. Seems like my darling dog discovered if she scratched at the bottom of the crate just right, she was able to literally able to inch the bottom of the crate until the entire tray was out. However, as clever as she was, she could not figure out how to dump the frame of the crate, hence allowing her to roam around the house with the crate on her back. Now I just knew Toby would never believe this mess happening again, so once again I left it for him to see it for himself. That was a Friday night, and the next morning it was decided that as much as we hated to, she was going to have to be penned outside while we were not at home. He was not too thrilled of mess he saw when he got home that night, and less thrilled we would have to keep her outside when we were not home, but he did agree we had no other choice.

That Friday night Toby sadly wandered outside to the backyard and took some measurement, drew out his plans for the dog yard, and headed for or local hardware store for the supplies he would need, hoping this was going to be the end of our problems.

Saturday morning came. Christy and TJ watched Toby working in the yard while he spent most of the day building a wonderful fourteen foot by fourteen foot enclosed dog yard and cozy four-foot dog house that any kid would kill for, as it resembled a small club house. And because our darling was a known escape artist, he laid a fencing floor camouflaged with pebbles and dirt so she could not dig her way out. By mid-afternoon it was finished and Christy was allowed to go inside of the pen and check it out. TJ in his toddler state thought the doghouse was great as he could go right inside it with the dog and stand up. He actually was a bit irritated with us when we picked him up and brought him back inside our house. We really thought this doggy yard would provide protection for our house and the dog while we were at work. She could get fresh air and wander around her yard, yet remain safe from harm, and so would our possessions.

Days, weeks, and months went by and Christy adjusted very well to being outside days when we were at work and inside when we were home. As she matured she was finally able to be left in the house for short periods of time like for shopping, and everything was actually left in one piece untouched. A year had gone by and Christy was due to have her first litter of pups. Since it was December, and since her due date was soon, I decided that I wanted to keep her inside for safety and warmth of her pups, as she continued to mature and her destructive ways had mostly subsided. Christmas eve she gave birth to thirteen pups, one being stillborn. I knew I would have to help her nurse her pups by supplementing the pups with some bottle feeding. The twelve remaining pups were healthy, happy, beautiful, and smart. She was a great mom, and they were so cute, but as the pups were growing their needs increased, like their needing exercise and training. They were outgrowing the kitchen and needed more room to romp and play. The weather was getting warmer and I started to bring the pups with their mom outside for short periods of time. At 5 weeks old I decided to start training them in the dog yard with her during the day while I was at work. At 8 weeks old they would soon be going to new homes, I hoped. They loved the smell of the fresh air, running on winterkilled grass, and were having great fun running in and out of the huge doghouse. They did well with their mom outside on a day we did not work, but I still wanted to do a test run when I was home just to see how well they would fare.

I knew I did not have to work they next day, so the plan was that when I got and after I showered, I would feed the dogs and put them out in the pen with Christy. I knew that I would be able to check on them every hour, and then I would bring them all back inside at the time when I normally would be coming home. The first three hours went well. I could see dog pen and the dogs from the porch, but they could not see me, and they all were doing great. While the pups were playing, Christy kept a watchful motherly eye on them. When they napped, she napped. So far so good it seemed. I couldn't have been more wrong!

About one pm my neighbor called to tell me he had just driven over Branch Street, the next street over parallel to ours on his way home, and he said he saw a silver and black German Shepard that looked like ours walking down the street with a litter of about a dozen puppies trailing behind her, heading towards Mains Street. This was not good! How could that be? I had just checked on the dogs not fifteen minutes before, and they appeared to all be sleeping. I quickly checked and sure enough they were all gone, but the outside gate of the dog yard was still securely closed. Now I was panicking. I grabbed my car keys and the sleeping toddler, put him in his car seat, and took a side street towards Branch. Sure as shooting there was that darn Christy walking down the street with all of her pups trailing behind her. I pulled the car over on the same side of the street as she was on, called her name and she literally stopped in her tracks looking for my voice. She was really happy to see me, and readily jumped into the car with me putting the pups right in behind her. It was a pretty tight fit with a mother German Shepard and her twelve pups fitting snuggly around a toddler in a car seat in a Firebird, who was giggling and only wanted to play with the puppies. Christy sat in the front street looking rather regal and barely looking at me, but occasionally giving me a glare that seemed to say, "I was only taking them for a walk." I actually found myself talking to the dog asking her how she managed to get out of the dog yard. Like she was going to answer me? Yeah! Right!

I pulled into our driveway, put a leash on Christy while my neighbor picked up TJ. The puppies of coursed followed their mom and me back out back into the dog yard. Christy readily went inside the dog yard as did all twelve of the pups. You would have thought they had been gone for days as they seemed happy to be back, and they all settled down and went to sleep.

An hour later I peeked out to see what was happening with the dogs, and there she was! I wanted to see what she was up to so I just stood quietly and watched. That sneaky Christy was literally climbing over the side of the pen, carefully and skillfully putting each paw through the fencing like a human climbing a ladder. Once at the top she sprung over the top and dropped to ground landing on all four feet. The jump never fazed her at all, and from her physic one could tell she was proud of what she just accomplished. Next she slithered to the gate, undid the slide bolt with her teeth, barked a very soft bark and literally let all the puppies out of the dog yard, and started up towards the house. I could not believe what I was seeing. I called to her and she eagerly started to run towards me as did the pups. My neighbor just snickered and said, "I told you she was a smart one. Guess you have to come up with plan B."

I brought the dogs into the house amazed at what I had just witnessed. Good thing the neighbor had witnessed it too because I was sure no one would believe the scenario had happened. Of course there were the people who lived on Branch Street and the traffic that saw Christy out with her pups who probably were all wondering who she belonged to and why was she free to wander with her pups. We definitely were going to have work on a plan B!

We had enough of the fencing left over to cap the entire dog yard in the cellar, and had discussed doing that when Toby first built the enclosure, but he thought because the fencing walls were so tall, we probably would not have had to go that route. Wrong! When Toby arrived home I told him what had happened and he agreed plan B had to go into effect that night. He told me he had been planning on doing that on the weekend anyway because he just had a gut feeling Christy was capable of figuring out an escape route. He called his dad on the phone and he agreed to help him with the capping. Christy was not happy with that plan, but she had a lifetime to get over it.

The next day my neighbor told me she howled and carried on throughout the day while we were gone because she could not make her escape, but she finally succumbed to the fact she wasn't going anywhere without our consent and settled down. She was mighty happy to go back into the house when I returned home that night and she played the role of the good dog thereafter; when we were home anyway.

The pups grew and by the time they were twelve weeks old they all had new homes. Christy missed her pups, but adjusted quite well when they were gone. Her destructive ways she never really outgrew, and she lived to be around twelve years old. She was such an affectionate and loving dog and even in her destructive ways I loved her dearly.

One of my favorite adventures I want to share before going on to my next adventure took place when Christy was six months old. I entered her into a point show mainly to see what potential she might have as a show dog. Unknown to me the breeder I purchased Christy from had also entered one of Christy's littermates, also a silver and black female, in the same show. You can imagine the look of surprise on both of our faces when we discovered we were both there. When each dog was called, we entered into the ring handling our own dogs, and we both were very surprised when the judge called both of our numbers for a final examination. The sister dog entered first and then Christy. Both dogs looked very regal, not moving a muscle while the judge was doing her final check. She examined the sister dog first and then came back over to Christy. The moment was tense while the examining was going on, but Christy being as Christy was; she did something I never expected her to do. Any dog person know that dogs live for the minute and you really never know what to expect all of the time with dogs, especially with puppies and strangers. The judge put her hand under Christy's lower jaw as if she was looking into her eyes, while taking her hand and gracefully rubbing her hand down Christy's back, when Christy very affectionally gently kissed the side of the judge's face. At that point I thought "so much for that. This whole event is over for us." Dog shows being dog shows when events like that take place, one never knows what the outcome might be, but I was almost certain we would be eliminated. To my surprise the judge slowly withdrew her hand from Christie's back while smiling, and called my number as number one and Christy's sister as number two. I was so surprised we went home with the first place for the best in puppy class for her breed. She competed against her sister three times after that, and each time walked away with the first place ribbon. Did she do the kissing thing each time? Yes she did. That girl was definitely a loveable sneak, and it almost looked like to me she knew exactly what she was doing. Good thing it was a different judge each time.

Toby, TJ and Klink

CHAPTER THREE
Colonel Klink Darling

Colonel Klink, or Klink as he was called, was a rescue dog. Someone Toby worked with told him about this German Shepard who was being mistreated and wondered if we might want to give him a home. We were told this dog's owner had mentioned in passing her kids had no time for him and she decided to just give him away, papers and all. We really were not looking for another dog, but after hearing his story, we decided we would at least go and look at him. I called the owner and she agreed on a time that was convenient for all, and after my dog classes one evening, we headed out to go get him. When we reached the destination it was not a pretty sight. There were a couple of horses, some cats and kittens, and Klink who was tied outside; all not in the best of living conditions, and all the animals were very thin. Klink appeared to be a black Shepard, not the silver and black color as we were told he was, and so thin you could literally count all of his bones. I was outraged and asked the owner how she could let his happen to these animals? He smelled so bad and looked so bad it was pathetic. I was wondering why no one in that area had reported this animal neglect to the authorities. She did not hesitate when I asked that she sign his AKC papers over to me, and almost seemed relieved he was going to another home. We put Klink in the car and left for home.

As Toby drove us home I read over his papers and I noticed he actually was one year old and registered as a silver and black German Shepard, again not the black color he seemed to be. He fell asleep five minutes on the road. Klink for all he had gone through was so laid back and gentle. The first thing we did when we got Kink home was to introduce him to Christy, feed him and schedule him to see the vet in the morning. Christy gave him the once over doggy fashion and walked away. She clearly was not impressed with this dirty, underfed, neglected dog we brought into our home.

I bathed him after he ate, and after the third shampooing, under all that dirt and neglect, and all the black fur he appeared to have started to turn to what was a beautiful Silver and black color. The muck and dirt that came out of his fur was unbelievable, but he seemed happy he was getting cleaned. He actually seemed to enjoy getting scrubbed in the tub as he never once tried to jump out, but licked my face occasionally while wagging his tail, and whimpered soft sounds of delight. Christy would wander into the bathroom once in awhile to see what was happening more out of curiosity I think, but you could see she still was not impressed with what she saw. After a final rinse, I dried him thoroughly, brushed him for almost an hour, gave him a new blue collar, and showed him where his sleeping place was going to be. He looked at me like he could not believe he was gong to be allowed to stay in the house. Because he was completely exhausted from his grooming, he quickly and quietly curled up next to a now sleeping Christy on the dog bed. She just raised her head, gave him a sniff and the once over again, and moved over so he could share the dog bed. Guess she like the clean version of Klink better than the dirty version. Within a few minutes both dogs were cuddled up to each other tightly and sound asleep. Thinking that went well, we went to bed totally exhausted. When I woke up in the morning, Klink was sleeping next to my side of the bed very peacefully and contently lying on the rug. He had accepted us.

I went downstairs and took the dogs outside for their morning chores, fed them, and then did my morning ritual of brushing them. Klink seemed happy with the brushing. German Shepards shed almost constantly and I felt they needed to be brushed on a daily basis to have them looking and feeling their best. Later that morning Klink and I headed out to see the vet. The vet was horrified to see him so thin, yet after examining him announced that he could be healthy again with food, exercise, and some TLC, and yes, it would take time, but it could be accomplished. I took him home, gave him the medication the vet had given me and evaluated him to see how much he knew for obedience training. I was amazed! Someone somewhere along down the line had spent time training this fellow. He knew the heel command, but we already knew this from the first night when we first brought him home. He also knew the long sit, the long stay, the come, and the down commands, and he held his head high as he readily did what he was asked to do, each time with such enthusiasm and love. I was impressed. Though he was thin, he continued wagging his tail as he moved through each command with grace and elegance, convincing me this dog did not set out in negligence. Something had happened along the way, but whatever it was, we would never know.

Days flew into weeks, weeks into months and Klink began to look and feel the picture of health again. His once bony, dull body now glistened with the silky, silvery and black fur he was supposed to have. His eyes were very clear. He was very affectionate, loyal, and protective, yet friendly and playful. When I felt he was ready, the day finally came when I took him and Christy to a point show in Albany, NY, agreeing to travel with a friend who was also showing her boxers at the same show. When we arrived at the show I closely watched Klink to see if he was showing signs of aggression or fear while getting prepared for the show. If he was feeling agitated, one would never have never known it. He seemed as relaxed as Christy was in her crate, like a dog that had done this before, dozing peacefully and ignoring everything around him. When his name and number were called to go into the show ring, he gaited proud and elegant, focusing only on me, his handler, while tuning out the surrounding background noise and the judge who was watching us compete. When the judge baited him for a final check, he stood so still looking regal and poised. You could have knocked me over with a feather when his number was called as the winner in the event. People were applauding, and my friend was jumping up and down going completely nuts. Klink had won the trophy and the ribbon for first place, which I never expected would have happened. I went to the judge, accepted the trophy and ribbon, and walked around the ring once more with Klink, and bent down to hug my dog. As I hugged him and kissed his head, that big old pink tongue gave me a big old slurp on my face as if to say "All I needed was a chance and you gave it to me."

Joyce later told me we were impressive as he moved with each command, and she said the look of love just radiated from each of us as we worked together in that show ring.

It was a mighty fine day; Christy won best in show in her division, Klink walked off with Best in Breed and Obedience, Joyce's dogs each won trophies and ribbons for their breed and divisions, and we were as giddy as school girls. But our excitement was interrupted abruptly.

While we were packing up and getting ready to leave, a man approached me, introduced himself as someone who had watched Klink grow up. He said he had had a hand in his basic training, but told me that he had noticed the dog started to look physically bad, and his owner had suddenly stopped going to classes three quarters through the program. He went on to say he knew this dog had great potential, and he had approached the owner with the possibility of private training or even purchasing him from them, but his offer was sharply declined. That was when they abruptly stopped going to classes and they would not return his calls. He learned in later months of Klink's fate and the other animals of neglect. He said even went to their house to see if he could maybe offer to take Klink off their hands, but the dog was already gone when he arrived there, and he was given no more information than that. He was very surprised and very happy to see this dog in better health and happily working in the show ring while he watched. I explained how we came to become the owners of Klink and said he was amazed what I had accomplished in such a short time frame. Klink wagged his tail eagerly when he saw the man, so I knew what he was telling me must be true.

The trip home seemed so much shorter than the trip to the show. Could it be because we both talked non-stop while the sleeping Boxers and Shepards seemed to be tuning us out? I am sure they were dreaming happy doggy dreams and couldn't have cared less what we were talking about.

When we got home, the look on our husbands' faces was priceless and the fact they were speechless was even better! The glory of the day was a great feeling of accomplishment, but deeply and truly all Klink ever wanted or needed, like all animals, was for someone to care for him and to love him for himself. He received that from us unconditionally and showed us so much love and affection in return for as long as he was with us. He didn't have to work or be a show dog. We took him out of a bad situation and gave him love and a chance to survive. He did what he did for us out of love, and he will always live in a special place in my heart.

Klink also became very special to the elderly neighbors who lived next door. Agnes and Baber Bill did not have any four-legged critters living there, only a bird they both loved dearly. Baber Bill would often sit outside in the early evening with a cocktail just relaxing. Other times he would crank up the grill and do a little cooking outside, often talking to the kids and dogs if they happened to be outside in the backyard playing. One evening he happened to have his evening cocktail in his hand, but decided to set it down on the nearby table that they kept near the back door entrance while he grilled their evening meal. Christy and Klink had been roaming around with the boys in the backyard when Baber Bill called the dogs over to give them each dog cookies from his stash he kept for the dogs. They each sat and offered their paws to shake hands as they were trained to do gently took the cookies and went to their respective places to eat them. After Klink ate his cookie, he got up slowly and walked over to where Baber Bill had left his cocktail, sniffed it and lapped up what was left in the glass. He then went back to lie down where he was previously. Agnes saw the whole thing happen as she was watching the kids play through her porch window. She said Klink was so matter of fact about the way he drank the drink, as if he always had an after-cookie cocktail. Baber Bill, unaware of what had happened, wandered over to where he had placed the drink on the table. He looked at the glass and muttered, "I must have drank it" as he popped what was left of the ice cube into his mouth and went into the house. Agnes said she never told him who drank his drink.

Being a manager of a local factory often took Baber Bill away for overnight business, leaving Agnes alone until he returned. Baber Bill unexpectedly had to go out of town on business one particular night, and asked us to keep an eye on the house for him, as he did not like leaving Agnes alone. That evening, for no apparent reason to us, Klink and Christy seemed very restless going to the side window and back door frequently and looking out that window. There was no barking or growling, no fur standing on end; just the unusual restless pacing of both dogs. Toby said something just did not feel right, but neither one of us could see anything out of the ordinary, but the two dogs were very restless. Half an hour later, Klink still was not able to settle down, and he went to the back door and started to softly growl while looking over at the garage where Agnes and Baber Bill parked their cars. I opened the back door looking through the screen door to see if I could see what was upsetting the dogs when all of a sudden Klink unexpectedly jumped through the screen door and ran over to the garage with Christy tight on his heels. It was at that point I told Toby I noticed the side door of the garage was slightly ajar where the two dogs ran inside. As I was speaking, you have never heard such a scream in your life coming from inside the garage. Toby ran next door and there was some man going through Agnes's car, as if he was looking for something to steal. I ran inside to tell Agnes what was going on and she called the police and reported the two German Shepards had a thief cornered in her garage. When the police arrived, the would be thief was more than ready to surrender to them. The dogs did not bite or bark at the man, they just stood there in a stance position showing him their teeth, making him very nervous and scared. He readily admitted he was going to steal some garden tools and loose change and cash Agnes might have had in her car, and had no idea the two dogs would be aware of his prescence.

The next night when Baber Bill returned home and learned what had happened in his absence, he was back outside grilling one of the biggest steaks I had ever seen. When he had it cooked to his standards, he put it on a platter, cut it into two equal portions, and instead of going inside his house, he came next door and gave Christy and Klink each a portion as a reward for a job well done. That night Agnes and Baber Bill ate hotdogs for supper.

Misty Moonlight

CHAPTER FOUR
Misty Moonlight Angel

It was 1979 and we had been dog less about six months and I just couldn't handle it any longer. Even with the two active and energetic boys, something was missing; a dog. The oldest son also had started hinting that the two boys also wanted a puppy. I had started reading with earnest the "For Sale" ads in our local newspapers. It was decided it was time to have another dog, but I wasn't sure what breed I wanted.

Be it angelic or heavenly intervention, one morning while reading the morning paper, I noticed an interesting newspaper ad that caught my eye. "FOR SALE BY OWNER: Doberman pups", it read. I thought about the newspaper ad for a few minutes and then made the call. The woman that owned the puppies was located in Pownal, and yes these pups were people-oriented and were almost ready to go to new homes, and both parents were on site. I made an appointment and told Toby where I was going and told him that he was welcome to come along. He declined saying he really knew nothing much about the breed, but respected my decision on the purchase. The two boys and me got in the car and headed for Pownal while they chatted about what color puppy they wanted, but neither one of the kids cared if it was a girl puppy or a boy puppy.

The directions given to me were easy and I soon found myself sitting in the driveway of the breeder. She greeted us, invited us in, and led us to where the daddy dog was. He was an absolute beauty; black and tan, very muscular, friendly, and one of the sweetest dogs you ever saw. The mother was just as sweet and friendly, and also a black and tan, taking to the boys right away. The pups were just simply wonderful; fat, playful, alert, and very social, and immediately came over to us and gently started licking the boys' faces and fingers. Then I spotted her and I picked her; my first mistake, as it was love at first slurp. We spent about an hour and a half there, while trying to make a decision about purchasing this female pup and also trying to figure out where I had seen or met this woman before. The boys were just having a great time playing with the puppies and telling Misty she was going to be their puppy. It looked like the boys had made a decision all by themselves about which puppy was coming home with us. Finally I asked this woman how I knew her? Come to find out she was also trying to figure out how she knew me? While talking, we discovered we had a mutual contact and had both taken obedience classes at the same time from the same instructor. A small world it is indeed as our mutual contact was also one of our neighbors who also had a pair of black and tan Dobermans. I put a down payment on the puppy and agreed to take her home in a couple of weeks. The kids were not happy they had to leave her, but they were happier when I handed them the tiny red puppy collar. They put it around her neck as they told her we would be back to visit in a couple of days. They got back in the car and talked non-stop about how cute the puppies all were, but how special our Misty was and how much fun we all were going to have with her. They couldn't wait to get back home and tell their dad all about this new puppy they had picked out, and they marked on the calendar in a bright red crayon the day when she could come home. Each morning the boys would take turns crossing off the day, and counting the days left until Misty would be coming home.

Two weeks flew by, and the day finally arrived for us to go pick Misty up and bring her home to meet the rest of her new family. The minute I brought her in the door, Toby fell in love with her. The boys took her and showed her around the house and took her outside to play in the backyard. She already had bonded with all of us and you could tell she felt at ease in her new environment and the doggy dad she met for the first time. While watching Misty interact with our family, I just had a sense that she was going to be one of the best puppies we have ever had. She did not prove me wrong.

After her last potty call for the first evening, our youngest son picked up the puppy and brought her upstairs to bed with him. I wanted to start crate training as soon as I could, but I have to admit I was thoroughly surprised when I went up stairs to get the pup only to see she had already fallen asleep cuddled up next to his chest on his bed. I stood there for a few minutes by his bed watching and trying to make a decision if I was going to pick up Misty and bring her downstairs to the crate, or to just let a sleeping dog lie. Both the boys and the puppy were sleeping so soundly I decided to leave her with the boys for the night. I put the gate in place at the top of the stairs so if she woke up during the night she would not be able to go downstairs and get into mischief. When I woke early up the next morning my first thought was "where is the puppy?" I got out of bed and was so surprised to see her still asleep on the bed curled up next to Paul, and no visible messes. "What a good girl" I thought. I gently woke her and picked her up to take her outside so she could do her bathroom chores when a small voice said "I already took her out once this morning, Mom. I woke up and had to go to the bathroom and took Misty out too, and she did real well. No messes inside. I gave her a cup of her puppy food and some water too." It made me feel so proud that a six-year-old child was able to make the decision to care for a new puppy when she needed it. "Good job" I said as I scooped her up and brought her downstairs and once again took her outside and brought her back inside to start the morning routine. Soon everyone in our house was up and the day began for us all.

Days went into weeks and weeks into months and everyone including Misty had adjusted to our normal daily routine. Unlike our wild Christy, this Misty was so laid back, as well as a real homebody, no crate was needed for her. She quickly learned she needed to stay in the kitchen when we were not home, and seemed quite content to do so. She had her toys and her favorite sneaker that one of they boys gave her when she first came home. It was actually a sneaker that the oldest had outgrown and just gave it to her to play with. It turned out to be her favorite toy, one that would last her an entire lifetime as she dragged that dirty old sneaker all over the house with her. It became her teddy bear; her comfort-zone toy. She even carried it upstairs with her and it lay next to her when she went to bed at night. It became very comical because whenever we planned a camping trip or a get-away, it was just second nature for her to pick it up and bring the sneaker along with her just like the boys would bring something they cherished.

But, as everyone knows, some dogs also have a lot of drool and of course the material in the sneaker soaked up the drool, along with the dirt and everything else it came in contact with, and she didn't seem to mind if the sneaker would get laundered from time to time. The comical thing was she would sit in front of the dryer waiting until it was dry and ready to play with again. It didn't matter if it was fifteen minutes or two hours, she would patiently sit and wait for its safe return. As time went on the sneaker became so worn and ragged to the point that all was left was the sole of the original sneaker, but try as we did, she would never accept a replacement and would actually howl and become very upset when we threw away that old thing. And every time we would give in and give her back "her sole" she would be as happy as a clam again. For years she still proudly carried the sneaker sole around as she did the first day it was given to her as a whole shoe.

From the first day I brought her home it was clear to see Misty was eager to learn and please her family. Obedience training and house-breaking came easily to her, and she hardly ever had any bathroom accidents. As her obedience training progressed, so did her confidence and ability to just carry out the commands given to her. By six months old she was so well trained I started thinking about showing her, but she was a part of our family and her being a show dog never entered my mind when I brought her home, so that thought was quickly placed in the back burner of my mind, and never resurrected again.

When Misty came home it was September and she grew as fast as the seasons changed. She really enjoyed spending time playing with the boys and the kids of the neighborhood and actually sometimes would just sit watching them as if to say "go ahead guys I got you covered." Just as she seemed she was always on guard watching and playing with the kids, she also proved how much she loved the boys.

It was mid-January of 1980 and the boys and some of the neighborhood kids were out in the backyard sliding down our little knoll in the fresh snow Mother Nature had deposited during the night. Misty took a couple of slides down the hill with the boys on their sleds when all of a sudden she took up her sentry duty watching them going up and down the hill. She watched cautiously as each child walked back up the hill hopping on his sled, and then back down the hill.

The kids were laughing and having so much fun and all seem to be going well, so I dashed inside the house just for a minute to grab some extra dry mittens and come right back out. As I was walking back towards where the boys were, all of a sudden Misty jumped up and ran like a bat out of hell down the hill. I couldn't imagine what had happened, but there was also a blood-curdling scream coming from down the hill, and I could only imagine the worst as I ran to see what was going on. It is amazing the pictures and thoughts that race through your mind as events like this are taking place; imagining the worst and hoping for the best scenario. I could also hear the kids screaming when I reached the crest of the hill. What I saw I could never have expected in a million years. There was Misty pulling Paul out of the river water back to the edge of the river with the kids trying to help her. She never stopped moving until she saw Paul was using his legs on the snow-covered ground. Apparently Paul's sled went out farther than it usually did, and he overshot the stopping point. He actually flew out onto the ice-covered river, and fell through the thinning ice. Misty must have sensed what was going to happen, because all the kids said she was out on that ice-covered river almost as fast as Paul fell through, grabbing his jacket-clothed arm and pulling him back to land before he had a chance to completely go under the ice. Misty was just seven months old and her instincts to protect were obviously very strong. That day she proved how much she loved those kids as well as being a valuable member of our family, willing to sacrifice her own life for a member of her family. All the kids were so glad she was there. One boy actually took off his coat and wrapped it around the shivering Doberman, scooping her up to keep her warm as we all ran back to the house. I scooped Paul up and ran in to the bathroom just off of the kitchen to get him out of the wet clothes, while throwing one of the boys a towel to rub dry Misty's thin wet coat and getting some warmth into her. While I stripped Paul out of his wet clothes and into some dry ones, I heard the kids singing, "For she's a jolly good fellow." I looked out into the kitchen only to see Misty wrapped in the towel and all the kids rubbing her fur dry and singing. I swear to God that dog was smiling. The minute she saw me she got up and walked into the bathroom looking for Paul, checking to see if he was okay. The kids all professed she was the best darn dog they ever knew.

Misty especially loved the beach, and she would get so excited when she saw the suitcases come out and me packing. The boys were allowed to bring one friend each with them for the beach trip as well as some toys, bikes, and kites etc. It was so funny watching the boys gather things they were going to bring with them as they helped us pack up the car for our trip. Misty always seemed to appear out of nowhere with her sneaker sole, as if to say " I have something to pack too." How the kids would all laugh as she assumed her space in the car and gently dropped that sole and actually lay down on it until we reached our destination. You can only imagine how odd we must have looked to other campers as we unloaded the car and set up our tent with two Dobermans in tow, and one who had a shoe sole as her luggage hanging from her mouth. I will tell you about the other Doberman a bit later, but the funny thing was, Misty just would sit and watch us going about setting up the campsite, and as soon as we were finished and told her it was okay to go into the tent, she always would go inside the tent, go to our sleeping bag where we slept and deposit her sneaker sole on top of the sleeping bag. She would never take it outside the tent while we were camping, and I think this was her way of making sure she had a little bit of home with her too.

One hot and humid evening at the beach, we took the two dogs and the four boys for a walk on the beach with a plan on stopping for ice cream on the way back to the campsite. It was low tide and the sunset was particularly beautiful that night, so the six of us sat on an old log just watching the boats while the sea gulls fished for food. The two dogs were running in and out of the ocean just doing their doggy thing, thoroughly enjoying themselves. I have said for years that animals can communicate with each other, and the next adventure once again confirms it. With no particular warning and for no reason that any of us could figure out, Misty and Clyde, who also had been sitting and watching the events as we were earlier before their romp in the water, looked at each other, jumped up and started digging sand and throwing it all around Toby's ankles. It was so funny we just decided to see how far they would go with the sand digging and throwing. How funny it was the two dogs were actually in sync, occasionally stopping to see how much sand they had dug up. When the sand was almost up to his knees, Toby just sat there quietly asking the dogs occasionally "Are you guys having fun?" as both dogs would stop digging and literally just lay down next to him, occasionally looking so proud of what they had accomplished. It was definitely a Kodak moment. When I sometimes take out the old photo albums we created along the years and I happen along those pictures I took that night, I always smile, more convinced dogs are just as capable of plotting and planning ways to have fun too, always living for the moment as dogs do.

Misty's loyalty and love for us was outstanding for the ten years she was with us. There are so many wonderful events and adventures we had with her that I will never forget, and as the kids said the cold January afternoon in 1980; she was truly one of the best darn dogs we ever had.

Clyde standing in the middle of junk

CHAPTER FIVE
Clyde Cadiddlehopper

It was a cool September afternoon in 1981 when Jack called to say his puppies had been born three days before, and he wanted us to come to his house and see them. I did not tell the boys about the pups, because Jack wanted to show them himself, but I made plans with Jack for the next day. The boys thought they were just going for a visit to see the horses and maybe be even get to play in the barn with his boys for awhile, or whatever adventures they managed to create while the adults visited. I still am not sure if they were even aware that Jack's Doberman, Misty's littermate, was expecting pups. They did know about the two dogs being sisters. We first met Jack at the breeder's purchasing a puppy for a companion dog the same day we picked Misty. Jack had been diagnosed with MS a few years earlier, and now in his mid thirties was already in advanced stages of the disease. In the past year he had become wheelchair-bound and completely dependent on other people, so a dog was a great companion while his wife worked and his boys were in school. He had help for a few hours a day while his family was away, but his dog helped fill the time when he was absence of human contact. Like Misty, this dog was loyal, sweet, and highly intelligent as well as attentive to her family, but especially to Jack.

When we arrived, all the boys were glad to see each other and Jack announced he had a surprise to show them, but first they had to help him push his wheelchair into the barn. TJ and Paul thought it great fun, an adventure, so they wasted no time pushing Jack while his boys ran ahead to open doors while we followed behind. The looks on their faces when they saw the puppies was priceless, as was their response when Jack winked at us, and his wife told them to pick one out, any pup they wanted, but only one. At first they though he was kidding, but when they were assured they were serious, they quickly chose a fat, wiggly black and tan male puppy they liked, and it was Paul who decided to name him Clyde Cadiddlehopper. All the boys unanimously decided it was a really cool name. Guess they all had been watching too much of The Red Skelton Show, but Clyde became the puppy's name. Jack, smiling as he spoke, gave our boys the little blue collar to tag the puppy, and warned them that they had to come and visit Clyde at least every four days so the momma dog knew they were going to take good care of her pup when we took him home. They were so excited planning for this puppy, and it was obvious that none of the adults were even a part of their thought process, so we left the boys in the barn with the puppies while we adults went to enjoy the rest of the warm autumn day on their deck.

Jack knew his time here on earth was getting short due to the fast advancement of his disease. We were all good friends, and he wanted our boys to have something to remember him by when he passed on, and felt that one of his pups was the ideal gift he could freely give with his heart. He knew the pup would have a good home, and watching the boys interact with the animals made him feel great. We agreed to honor his request.

We dutifully went to visit every four days and the weeks quickly flew by to the day when we would bring Clyde home. When we brought Clyde home, I introduced Misty to the puppy, and was completely surprised by Misty's rejection of the puppy. Instead of licking and nudging the pup, Misty literally looked me in the eye, turned, and walked upstairs ignoring us all. I immediately knew something was wrong and I could not let her walk out of the room that way. I told the boys to take Clyde outside and play with him for a few minutes, which they eagerly did. I immediately went upstairs to where Misty was lying on our bed with her great head resting on her front paws. She did not even look at me when I walked into the room. She looked so forlorn and lost like she had lost her best friend, and in this case probably her family. I thought "her feelings are hurt. She is broken hearted about the puppy." I walked over to the bed, sat down beside her and started to pet her as I gently spoke to her.

"What's the matter girl? Why are you so sad?" She would not look at me, but turned her head away from me looking out the nearby window. Whoever said dogs don't have feelings was dead wrong. It was very clear Misty was broken-hearted about this puppy coming into her home unannounced. I continued to stroke her softly while speaking to her. "Don't you like Clyde? He's just a puppy. You are good with other dogs. You know we love you and Clyde is going to be part of the family, and we love you just as much. We always will love you because you are our girl."

She wasn't buying this extra love stuff from me at all. She had been the dog queen in her home for two years and now a sniffling, fat puppy had entered her kingdom and she was not about to share it with another dog. I knew she would eventually give in, but I needed to give her a bit of space, so I went downstairs to the kitchen and left her on the bed. Within fifteen minutes she came slinking down the stairs and quietly came up next to me and nudged me gently on my hand as I pretended to read the paper. I slipped my hand down and petted her head while turning to look at her saying "Its okay girl. You will get use to him and you might even like him in time. Love him even. By the way, his name is Clyde." She actually was peeking through the door as I spoke watching the boys playing with Clyde.

Just as I was finished talking to Misty, TJ came bounding in the back door unaware I was talking to Misty, but gleefully saying while taking her collar gently and taking her outside with him "Misty come on girl. Come play ball with Clyde and us. He's new and you gotta show him how it's done. He needs you Misty. He doesn't even know what a

Frisbee is yet." She was so taken off guard, she went willing and quickly out the back door with him. I went outside too, watching to see what might happen next with Misty and the puppy, aware that I might have to intervene if she decided to hurt the pup.

She sniffed the pup while she looked around to see if anyone was watching her. She nudged the pup with her nose. She looked around. She licked him on the face, checked out his privates, and sniffed his butt while holding him in place with her paw. She looked around, and then suddenly the chase was on.

She grabbed the ball, ran a few feet, bowed down and threw her rear end up in the air, and softly barked as if to say "Come get it kid." Fat, little Clyde waddled over to her. She dropped the ball. She batted it to him and quickly grabbed it again and the chase was back on. She was quick, but gentle and very loving to him. Not once did she show any kind of aggression towards this puppy. It was obvious she had accepted the pup, and he her, and she was back to her lovable sweet self. You could see both dogs were enjoying themselves, as were the two boys. I continued to sit on the back step and watch the boys and the dogs thinking this was going to work. Misty was happy, the boys were happy, and the puppy happy, and all seemed to be adjusting well.

First night with a new puppy in the house went real well. The boys were a bit older and had been involved with the care of Misty, so they were familiar with a routine and automatically started teaching Clyde the routine the first night in our home. Watching the two boys talking to Misty and Clyde and how the dogs responded to the boys was priceless. They just chatted away to the dogs and each other as if they had been buddies all their lives, not as a person to a dog, but as friends. It was so interesting watching Misty interacting with this puppy, often nudging the pup along if he did not seem to be moving fast enough, because he often got side-tracked as puppies do, very much like kids do when they discover something new. It was so funny watching the boys literally picking up Clyde the puppy and placing him where they wanted him to be, only to see him get that "If you think I'm staying here, you can guess again" look on his puppy face, and to see him take off like a bat out of hell with both of the boys and Misty running after him across the yard. Clyde sure did have a lot of energy and determination for an eight-week-old pup; a quality we really admired as he grew and matured.

After the last call of nature for the dogs and the boys that night, it was quickly noticed what dog was going to sleep where. Squatter's quarters were well established by the boys while they were getting ready for bed while the dogs looked on. TJ called Misty to come to him and Paul picked up the little fat Clyde as well as they ascended the stairs, the boys chattering to the dogs all the way up the stairs. Misty immediately jumped on TJ's bed while Paul put Clyde on his bed, and the puppy instinctively crawled into a tight ball right next to Paul. They all fell asleep almost immediately, all exhausted from a busy and fun-filled day. So much for plan A. Clyde like Misty was such a good puppy he never needed or used a crate.

When we went up bed later that night, it was as if they were all statues, unmoved from their earlier positions, and soundly sleeping. There was an angelic look about Clyde as he slept, but I just sensed this puppy was not going to be the angel he appeared to be.

Misty just looked up and gave me the once over as I kissed TJ goodnight, Paul never moved, and Clyde was still curled up tightly to Paul as he had been earlier while he was passing silent-but-deadly bodily emissions as he slept, something he would do all his life. Toby laughingly said, "We better crack a window open a bit so no one dies from asphyxiation during the night." The sun rose again in the morning and everyone was still alive and well, while Clyde continued to fart! I never had a puppy that had gas like that, but thinking once he was established on a routine and regular diet, that would pass. I was so wrong!

I called Misty and picked up the puppy and started our morning routine, and everything seemed to be going okay. This was the morning I discovered that fat little Clyde had been born with a bit of trickery in him, something he would do all of his life.

I took the dogs outside to do their bathroom chores, and all of a sudden Clyde just seemed to have disappeared in clear view. I actually could not see him and panicked as I called his name repeatedly hoping he would appear. He did not. "Where did he go, Misty?" I asked, like she was going to answer me. Misty just sat there looking at me like I was some kind of fool that had lost her mind. I must have wandered around that cursed yard for twenty minutes looking for that puppy with Misty making no effort to get up from her sitting position, but just sat there all that time just watching me before I realized that sneaky Clyde had some how slithered behind me just out of sight, and was literally walking in my footfalls as I walked. When I turned around and saw him, he just assumed the same position as Misty staring at me while wagging his tail as if he was saying, "Ha ha I fooled you." I looked at Misty and said "That's not funny. You two scared me. I thought Clyde was lost." Misty ignored me, got up, nudged Clyde, gave me a dirty look, and they both walked up the steps to go inside. Misty had obviously assumed the mother role and was showing Clyde the ropes.

When I went inside and fixed their food, both dogs were patiently sitting watching me while I mixed everything together for their meal. Clyde had no idea what I was doing, but he just continued to sit there and mirror whatever movement Misty would make. "What a pair", I thought. At least Misty was happy again and had accepted the puppy. The minute I put the dog food dishes down, Clyde literally dove and jumped in the middle of his dish, like a mad piranha that had not eaten for a week, spewing food everywhere. I never had seen a dish of puppy food disappear so fast. There he sat in the middle of the food dish chomping away. Those little puppy jaws loaded with shark-like puppy teeth were literally chomping away as fast as they could go consuming every morsel of food. Once finished eating, he slowly waddled out of the dish while licking his lips and picking up the crumbs he had strewn about with his dinner dive. Then he started stretching his little body expelling the loudest burp and puppy fart at the same time that I had ever heard. I never knew a puppy fart could have a slight whistle to it. I just could not move, but stood there in amazement with no one else to share this moment that I had just witnessed. It was hard to believe that a puppy of that size could consume his food that fast, followed by such loud noises. Misty was so shocked hearing the noises coming from that little fat, black body, she literally stopped eating, cocked her head as if to say "What on earth is that racket?" as she curiously walked over and sniffed the pup. The cat headed for the high country (upstairs) as if she had been shot out of a cannon. When Misty was satisfied Clyde was okay, she finished her meal, occasionally glancing at him as if in disbelief such sounds could come from such a small body. Clyde just sat there unconcerned to what we had just witnessed. Unknown to me that this was going to be the morning routine I came to call "the Clyde Factor."

Clyde was a very intelligent dog, was eager to learn new things, very friendly and loving as well as loyal, but no one was immune from his trickery. One of the things he did was what we called the "bush whack." If he even suspected he was not your center of focus and you were not paying enough attention to him, he would start running circles around his intended victim, making the circles smaller and smaller until he was right behind your knees. And then with no warning he would whip that big old butt of his against the back of your legs, dropping you to your knees like a ton of bricks. Unless you knew the dog and his trickery, you never knew what happened or how you got on your knees so fast. Mission accomplished, he would just sit down out of reach, looking at you like he was laughing at what had just taken place. One never knew when or where he would strike. One minute he was a very loving, laid back dog looking regal and being good, the next minute he was like some ninja on a mission for search and destroy. Good thing people who became the victim usually laughed when they discovered what had happened. You had to love Clyde. He was like a clown in a Doberman costume.

Another thing he would do was to hide things on you, and I became the subject more than once to this madness. The first time he did the "hide and find" thing he was about eight months old.

I had finished some baking, taking the pan of brownies out of the oven and placed the oven mitts on the kitchen counter instead of hanging them up before I walked off to do something else. Misty and Clyde were lying under the kitchen table sound asleep, occasionally twitching their noses as if they were just sniffing the aroma of the brownies, or so I thought. On my way back into the kitchen the thought fleeted through my mind that I needed to hang up the oven mitts. I glanced at the counter; no mitts. I surveyed the kitchen; no mitts. I looked at the dogs; both were still asleep, or so I thought. "Now where on earth did I put those oven mitts?" I thought. I happened to look back under the table and noticed Clyde was half looking at me, but seemed to also be half asleep, so I basically ignored him and started to look around, searching for and wondering where I could have left those oven mitts. Toby was refinishing a gun stock so I asked him if he had seen the mitts. He did not, but announced the brownies sure smelled good and he wondered if they needed to be tested. I ignored him and continued my search. I must have searched for over an hour with no luck in finding them, thinking I must be losing my mind, but figured they would turn up eventually; things usually did. The dogs were still under the table unmoved, so I went outside to see what the boys were up to when Toby came to the back door.

"Hey Judy, did you happen to pick up the roll of fine steel wool a few minutes ago?"

"No, why, is it missing?"

"Yes. It was like it just disappeared. I went down cellar to get something and it was gone when I came upstairs. Like it just plain vanished."

"Are you sure you didn't drop it under your work table?"

"I looked. Not there, not anywhere. It's like we have a ghost and it disappeared."

"Like the oven mitts did. It seems like there is a lot of disappearing going on around here today."

The dogs did not move and they did not acknowledge our presence of talking, except for Clyde who very slightly raised his ears and looked away like he was changing his comfort mode. We both went on doing whatever it was we were doing, oblivious to the fact Clyde was the culprit.

I asked the boys if they for some reason had seen or taken the oven mitts and they had not. It just kept bugging me that those darn mitts had disappeared. The dogs still had not moved. As I walked back into the kitchen, I spotted one of the dogs' tennis balls. I picked it up and casually threw it into the dog basket of toys, watching it sail past what appeared to be the still two sleeping dogs. In a flash Clyde was on all fours diving into that basket looking for that ball, and Misty, who had been peacefully asleep, looked as if she had been run over by a freight train. Clyde's legs had gotten caught on Misty's sleek body and literally spun her around so she actually was facing the opposite direction, looking a bit confused and out of sorts. The oven mitts went flying across my feet as did the steel wool.

"Found them," I said.

"Found what?" Toby asked

"My oven mitts and your steel wool. Seem like Clyde must have stolen them and was laying on them. He's done it again; he's pulled another trick on us."

Two mysteries solved. Score: Clyde 2 Judy 0 Toby 0. Not a bad score for the day for the dog.

Like Misty, Clyde loved the beach and loved to splash around in the surf for what seemed an eternity. It was very entertaining watching the two dogs trying to catch the foamy waves with no luck. They would do this for long periods of time. Clyde also loved sticking his head under the water and pulling out of the water whatever he could get his choppers on, and it didn't matter if it was seaweed, driftwood, old shells, or whatever. If it moved in the water, it was fair game and it was bound to end up in his mouth.

One hot July afternoon, Clyde decided to do his diver dog thing and I heard a terrible yelp almost as fast as he stuck his head under the water. My first thought was he had gotten hurt and I quickly dashed out to the surf where he was to see if he was okay. He was also running towards me as fast as his legs would carry him. I couldn't believe what I was seeing. Attached to his upper lip was a small crab, the size of a quarter, and it had no intentions of letting loose. Clyde had finally met his match as he tangled with a sea creature that probably did not want to be on his lip any more than he wanted it there. I felt bad for the dog, and he looked so strange with the tiny crab attached to his lip. There was no blood or visible wound that I could see. He sat so still, resting his head in my hands while I looked at him to see how I could get that crab off from his upper lip. The dog was in obvious pain, but remained calm. The crab would not let go no matter what I tried, and as the dog's lip started to swell, I started to worry.

I continued to cradle Clyde's wet, black head in my hands while his beautiful brown eyes met mine. "You got yourself into a good mess this time boy. I hope I can get this thing off your lip."

I still couldn't budge that crab no matter what I did, yet the dog remained quiet while I worked on him, emitting only an occasional soft whimper. As I was thinking I had to get this dog to a vet, a man who was fishing in the surf noticed I was obviously having a problem and came over to see if he could help. He took one look at Clyde and the crab, checking out the situation with an intense gaze. He spoke softly and reassuringly to Clyde, gently cradling his great head while his large hands were manipulating the crab's claws that had pinched shut on the dog's lip. In a blink of an eye he had that crab off of Clyde's lip with no lacerations noted, but his lip was so swollen by this point he looked like he had been beaten. I thanked the man for helping me, and he thanked me for the fishing bait.

Later on that afternoon as the man was walking past our campsite, he stopped to inquire how Clyde was doing. Clyde and Misty were peacefully lying inside the screen house asleep; Misty looking regal and Clyde still looking as if he had gone a few rounds in the boxing ring, but none-the-less for wear. The man gently and tenderly patted them both with much affection while each one of the dogs continued to rest.

"By the way, thanks for the bait. Thanks to your dog I have supper tonight."

He then showed us the fish he caught on that tiny crab. Clyde opened his eyes for a moment and gave him the most disgusted look and then closed his eyes again as if to say, "If I don't see you, you don't exist."

As Clyde grew and matured, the boys, Clyde and Misty were all mostly inseparable. Where you saw the kids, you saw the dogs. Clyde hardly ever left Misty's side for long, and this companionship lasted for all the days of their lives. That is with one exception; Clyde was nearly full-grown when we had this beautiful black and white Angora cat that had been given to us and he fell in love with her too, almost immediately. The dogs and cat all played and romped. She washed them; they washed her, and all the animals slept together at times. What we did not know was this cat was pregnant when she was given to us. To make a long story short, she gave birth one evening in our closed-in sun porch, and Clyde just happened to be out there when the kittens were being born. Now how many adult cats do you now of that will let a male dog near her when she is giving birth? Well, Spunky did. She would even let the dogs lay next to her while she nursed and cared for her babies, but the funny thing was, when she wanted to go outside to do her bathroom chores, or go to her feeding place to eat, she would meow and Clyde would always go out and sit with her kittens. It was the cutest darn thing you ever saw. Here was this 120 pound Doberman lying on the floor with six kittens cuddled up to his belly like they were going to nurse. He arranged his back feet so they were touching his front feet, creating a great big circle to keep the kittens in one place. As they grew and started to try and wander from the circle, he would gently pick the offender up and put thim back in his circle, and he would stay there with those babies until Spunky returned. And he was not afraid to give those kittens a gentle wash with his tongue. I really think he missed the kittens more after we found new home for them than Spunky, the mother cat did

One very cold February night his world was shattered. Misty was sleeping on the dog bed and Clyde was cuddled up to her, when Clyde suddenly jumped up as if he had been shot or had a bad dream. He was soaking wet, and smelled of urine. He sniffed the sleeping Misty all over and then himself, and proceeded to try to clean up the urine-soaked dog bed. He obviously could not, and Misty was not moving. I checked to see what was happening. Our aging Misty had obviously had a stoke and was not able to stand or use her back legs, and had lost all function in her back end. Her breathing was heavy and we knew what we feared was happening; our aging Misty was dying. Poor Clyde was trying his best to revive her, to no avail. We knew this was going to happen eventually, but it seemed too quick a time frame to be happening now, and we still were not ready. Misty died that night and I really think part of Clyde died that night too. We buried Misty under the lilac tree where Clyde and Misty would often lay and watch the neighborhood activities and nap outside.

He was two years younger than Misty, but since her death his energetic self just was not there. He was literally mourning her death. He ate very little, and little by little no longer showed any interest in his toys, and only half-heartedly wanted to go anywhere with anyone. When we would go for walks, I am sure he only went with me because he knew I wanted him to. On the walks he no longer would sniff around trees and things where he use take his frequent whizzes, marking everything with his scent as we walked. He very seldom turned his head and looked up at me like he use to do, but kept his gaze focusing on what was ahead of him. It was like he was wishing we could just turn around and go home. He slept a lot. He was getting very thin as he hardly was eating now no matter what we would offer him to eat. He would often go outside and just lie on Misty's grave like he was trying to communicate with her. He seemed depressed, and I was very worried about him. It was very hard losing Misty for all of us, and I didn't want to lose him too.

I took him to the vet and she agreed he was grieving, and could die if he could not turn it around. No matter what we did, Clyde was obviously very lonely and sad without Misty, and just did not want to live without her. I had heard this sometimes happens with animals that are raised together, but I never thought I would have to watch this happen to one of my animals. It was so hard watching him live this way, and it was even harder to accept he had given up wanting to live. Sadly, our wonderful Clyde died exactly six months to the day Misty died, and I know he died of a broken heart. We buried him next to Misty under the lilac bushes where they will always be together.

The Red Dog laying in one of his haunts

CHAPTER SIX
The Red Dog

Now we come to The Red Dog. It is a bittersweet story about this dog, but not a totally bad one. I have to admit he was not one of my favorite all-time dogs, in fact he was a dog most people either liked and tolerated, or you just plain did not like him at all. He actually had a personality that most people could not stand, and he barely tolerated any humans or any other animals at all. Basically he would not attach himself to any human or animal long-term. Like one of my sisters said one day, he was a true psycho dog; one minute he could be very loving giving you kisses and letting you pet him, the next second he was running behind the couch barking up a storm for no apparent reason anyone could figure out. He had never been abused to our knowledge, and he basically was just one of those dogs who were not well-balanced by today's standards. Maybe it could have been the mixture of his breeding. The Dog Whisperer would have had a real challenge with this one dog had he been around at the time!

It all started one afternoon when my husband and his cousin were heading to work when his cousin noticed a sign that advertised **Free Beagle Puppies**. Now you know people just are not going to be giving away purebred dogs unless there is a catch in the deal. And if it sounds too good to be true it usually is, as the old saying goes. Anyway they stopped and inquired about the puppies because the cousin was looking for a Beagle puppy. Why? Who knows? That's just the way it was. Anyway, they stopped, looked, and the next thing Toby knew they were heading home after they finished work with a really cute, so called Beagle- looking puppy with no AKC papers, sitting in his lap while his cousin drove home. "Good deal it was; he was a free puppy."

Toby said the lady who owned them was all too eager to have the puppies go to new homes, and the mother dog was not available to view. She never asked them any questions, but was rather pushy about getting rid of all the pups. I tried to tell both of them that this seemed like a red-flag deal to me. Something appeared to be very wrong with the whole picture, and it could be these pups were not purebreds, they were stolen, or there was something wrong with the litter genetically speaking. I was going with the idea they were not pure breds as advertised. I knew time would tell the facts, but then again sometimes you just cannot make people (like some men I know) see the handwriting on the wall; you have to just sit back and wait, as sometimes people just need to find out things for themselves.

Time went on and The Red Dog, as he became to be known, grew, and started to develop some odd characteristics. He was very moody; a definite red-flag warning in dog standards of today, and all of a sudden he grew a beard like a Terrier. I just had a feeling he was not a purebred Beagle when he first arrived at our house prior to the growth of his facial hair, and his moodiness explained a lot once we saw that little beard develop. He wouldn't so much pick fights with other dogs, but Toby's cousin's other dog just plan did not like him either right from the start, and she was a wonderful friendly dog. Toby's cousin tolerated the moodiness of this dog for about four months, and then his cousin asked him one day on the way to work if we could take the dog and see if we could work with him. I was very leery about this request, but Toby agreed to take him for a trial period to see if we could train him. That trial period lasted thirteen years.

The first night at our house I just knew this was a mistake. Misty and Clyde took an instant dislike to him as did the cats, and the cats never did like him. In fact, the cats completely avoided him whenever possible. The two Dobermans didn't hurt him or fight with him; they just kept their distance. Basically all the other critters just tolerated his presence as well. He would not play with the others and sometimes would actually just walk away like he did not want to be bothered with any of them, anything, or anyone. He would not play with the kids at all. He would only let allow a human to pet him when it was convenient for him. He would not play with any of the dog toys. He would sometimes growl and bark at his food dish, and nobody could figure out why. We were feeling so bad that he seemed so unhappy and couldn't figure out what to do for him. No one could.

Sometimes he would go willingly for a ride in the car with me, but those were rare times. He liked go for walks with me on the leash, and he would barely acknowledge the presence of the other dogs if they tagged along too. He basically was happier if we were alone or with the horses. For some reason the horses seemed to understand him better and they actually got along better with him whenever they greeted each other. They were actually sometimes playful with him and it was actually enjoyable and nice to watch them all interact. But even these happy moments with Red and the horses did not last for long. As most people know, horses are very good judges of personality and characters, and maybe they just understood Red better than anyone else.

As odd as he was, he was really cute looking, especially with that beard of his and his bushy eyebrows. People used to kid Toby whenever they would see the both of them together and say Red Dog and he looked alike. We really did try to give him a good home, and I hope for the most part he was happy with us. When he was about thirteen years old he died very peacefully. Hopefully this little manic dog finally found true happiness crossing over the Rainbow Bridge.

Harley

CHAPTER SEVEN
Harley Davidson Dawg

The death of Clyde took a toll on us all, and we decided not to purchase have any other dogs for a while. The house seemed so empty as I put all Clyde's things away, and my heart was broken once again.It seemed like something was missing in our lives. There was no furry creature nudging your hand while you watch TV or curling next to your feet. Red avoided us except when it was time to eat. I missed the companionship of a loving dog as I walked along our road. My morning routine seemed like mechanical movements with no meaning. Toby had also had a near-fatal heart attack and was recovering at home and was alone much of the day when I worked, and I was uncomfortable about that. The Red Dog sure was not much company for anyone. At forty-two years old, he was too young to be recovering from a heart attack and being alone most of the day. Toby also mentioned in passing one day that it would be nice someday to have a Labrador Retriever to keep him company during the day, but he never pressed the issue.

One morning when I was reading the morning paper, I saw the newspaper ad for Labrador puppies, and on the spur of the moment my oldest son and I went to see them. Toby had no idea where I was headed. When Rachel led us to where the puppies were playing, suddenly there he was. One fat yellow ball of fur going in and out through a screened porch while playfully shaking his little blond head to and fro with a piece of foam rubber in his mouth that he had chewed off the cushion from the nearby couch. One of the pups had pulled the cushion down off of the couch and claimed it for his very own. The yellow fur ball seemed to be on a mission of having the time of his life going in and out of that section of screen on the porch, never once dropping the foam rubber. Once he spotted us, he came over to us and pushed the piece of foam rubber in TJ's hand as if to say "Here take this. I want you to play with me." He was so friendly and loving live wire, a beautiful color, and I knew he was meant to be ours.

"This is the one Mom," TJ said picking up the puppy to examine him. I don't know what came over me, but I bought him on the spot. He was only six weeks old and not yet fully weaned, so I knew I had a couple of weeks to get prepared for him. I decided he would be an early Christmas present for Toby, but we would keep him a secret until I could bring him home. We named him Harley Davidson Dawg, and why that name, I have no clue. It just sounded good. I told Rachel this puppy was a surprise, so she agreed she would call me at night after I was home from work when he was ready for his new home, and we came up with a secret code word she would use to let me know I could come and get Harley. Oh the thrill of a secret purchase! We were going to have a really nice dog again, and maybe that Red Dog would come around and be civil.

On my way home I stopped and bought a bag of puppy food and a new red collar for Harley. I decided to keep these secret purchases in the trunk of my car until the day I would bring him home.

Two weeks later, a Thursday night, Rachel called me in code telling me she had something of mine I needed to pick up. Toby was watching TV, so I told him I had to go pick up the "goods" and would be right back. He nodded, too engrossed in what he was watching, so I left and went to pick up Harley. Being a man and devoted to what he was watching, he had no clue what I had told him.

When I arrived at Rachel's there were also other people there who were picking up their new pups. I felt bad for the mother dog loosing most of her babies the same night, but Rachel assured us she was spacing the puppies so the mother dog would adjust to their departures just fine.

I gathered Harley up, put his new red collar on him, and headed for home. I knew almost immediately he was going to be a cuddle bug when he scooted out of the box from the passenger seat on to my lap in the driver's seat. So much for Plan A and that box I planned on bringing him home in. He stood up in the box with his little front legs hanging over the top looking at me as he panted and wagged his tail. He actually gave me the look that said "If you think for one minute I'm staying in this thing, there's no way pal I am. I want out and I want out now. I'm on a mission too and it's not going to be in this box!" as he scooted over the top of the box and right into my lap. It was a good thing we had only a less than fifteen-minute ride home because this Harley Davidson Dawg was just too busy getting more acquainted to even think about sleeping. He chewed on my fingers, he licked my arm and chin, he changed positions in my lap at least a half a dozen times, he sniffed the air, and he looked out the window making soft grunting noises as if he already missed his litter mates. Nevertheless we arrived home safely and soundly, entering through the back driveway so Toby would not hear me when I pulled in the yard. I walked in the laundry room and headed for the living room where that same TV show was on.

"You weren't gone long. Must have been a fast transaction," he muttered as he continued to watch his program, unaware by now I was standing in the doorway with a yellow Labrador Retriever puppy in my arms. The Red Dog spotted me and darted behind the couch where he almost always would retreat when something did not go his way. All of a sudden Toby looked up and the look of surprise on his face was priceless.

"Toby I want you to meet Harley Davidson Dawg" I said as I handed him the wiggling ball of yellow fur. "He sure has a lot of energy. He is eight weeks old, he is your early Christmas present, and I don't want to hear another word about it."

The Red Dog just stayed behind the couch as Toby took the wriggling ball of yellow fur from me and his eyes welled up with tears saying, "Well hello there Harley Davidson Dawg. Where did you come from? I have always wanted a Lab puppy and now we have one Thanks Honey. I bet you were the mission your new mom here went on. What a great surprise! Red you better get use to him. He is staying."

Red never moved or did anything, but stayed behind the couch. The puppy was now doing the smelling things dogs do when the meet someone new, and he planted a series slobbery wet kisses right across Toby's face.

"You sure are a lovable little guy. I think you are going to fit in just right here" Toby said, by now completely ignoring the TV show he just had to watch earlier before I left to get the pup.

It was still early evening with the sun still up when we took Harley outside and began to show him around his new home. The Red Dog refused to join us. All of a sudden the puppy spotted our cat was who was walking across the yard towards us, and she saw him just about the same time. "This is going to prove interesting," we both said as we watched the scenario starting to take place.

The cat was a lot bigger than Harley, but when she saw him coming towards her, she huffed herself up, hissed, spit, and carried on as if to say "Where the hell did you come from and who the hell are you?"

They collided with each other head on, rolling around on the green grass in the backyard; Harley trying to be friendly puppy style while that darn cat just kept on a hissing and a spitting. I have to admit we were so amazed that she never once made any physical contact on the puppy with her claws opened. Next came the standoff.

Old Fluffer had no clue where this puppy came from. All she knew is one minute she was walking toward us glad to see us, the next minute she was being tackled by a midget, yellow, furry dog who was slobbering all over her and seemed to be pushing her around while she hissed, spitted, and carried on about his being in her backyard. Her usually well-groomed fur seemed to be very wet from the dog slobber and sticking up all over while going in all different directions. Fluffer looked startled while Harley looked just fine. His tail kept wagging and you could see he wanted to play, while Fluffer clearly did not. After a few minutes of this introduction, the half-dazed Fluffer took her paw and planted it right in the middle of Harley's head, pushing him into a sitting position and each animal looking eye to eye with each other as if Fluffer was trying to say "Okay kid I get the message. You are glad to meet me, but I am not too thrilled to meet you, but you are here and let's make the most of it!" She half turned and looked at us as if to say, "I will deal with you two later. I liked being the only good animal. Now I have to train another dog all over again!"

She literally stomped her grey and white feet while shaking here plume-like tail as she was going into the house, every few steps making hissing noises, all the while shooting us her infamous dirty looks. Harley could have cared less; this fur ball was moving and it had spunk, and he wanted to play.

The funniest thing was when Fluffer walked into the living room and saw the doggy toy box had been refreshed with a few new toys along with some of the older ones. When she first discovered the doggy toy basket was back in its old familiar spot, she actually did a double take, shooting me at once one of her best dirty looks ever, but then she walked over to it closer as if to say "I hope I am not seeing what I think I see. Are those new doggy toys?" Red Dog continued to stay behind the couch out of sight.

This cat was the queen of giving dirty looks when she was provoked, and she now was really right on the edge of being beyond provoked. First there was a new puppy in her yard, and now this doggy toy basket has new toys in it, and that yellow fur ball looks like he is staying in her house. She was not happy!

It really was a priceless moment as she suddenly realized something got past her when she was outside. But, being nosy as she was and not wanting anything to get past her, she slowly walked up to the basket like she was stalking something, sniffing it as she walked, while every now and then continued throwing us humans one of her infamous "dirty-looks". She was so focused on the basket she had no idea Harley was silently followed her, sniffing her footfalls as she slowly walked up close to the basket. Once the mission of walking up to the basket and checking out the new toys was completed, she stopped, sat down looking the basket thing over, and hung her head as if to say "I just cannot believe they brought another dog into my house. I guess this means it is going to stay. Now I have to train another dog!" Her dirty looks continued as she hung her head even lower as if she was in deep thought, like she was plotting something; "How do I get rid of it?" She suddenly looked behind the couch at The Red Dog and he just backed in further as if to say, "Don't even think about asking me to help you!"

Fluffer, now disgusted too with the Red Dog, walked back over to the dog toy basket and just sat down pouting. By now Harley was sitting next to her also peering into the basket to see what she was looking at and what was in there. At the same moment they turned and looked at each other. Fluffer, being shocked that the puppy had snuck up on her, (the nerve of him) and it must have been a feeling of shell shock, because Fluffer went straight up in the air and straight down again spitting, hissing, yowling, and literally landed in the toy basket. Harley just sat there looking at us and back again at her, not moving from his spot, cocking his head as if to say "What was that all about?"

Poor Fluffer cat. She was so upset when she noticed Harley leaning his head into the basket sniffing around she literally made the leap of faith, jumped over Harley, and ran upstairs where she stayed until we went to bed.

Now what Fluffer did not know was that upstairs next to our bed was a box with a blanket in it where Harley was going to sleep. You can only imagine the look or horror on her sweet face when I walked into the room to put Harley down for the night, and I discovered the cat in the box. First she gave me a look of surprise, followed by a "No way are you putting him into this box with me" look. She had found that box fair and square and she thought she was claiming it for her own. Wrong!

I decided since she would not budge and because I had an armful of puppy and couldn't manage both taking one cat out and putting one puppy in the box, I would just put the puppy in with the cat. Oh, she hissed and meowed and carried on, but again never made any attempt to hurt Harley. Tired out by now, Harley just ignored her, curled up in a ball and fell asleep. Fluffer looked at me as if to say "Oh what the heck!" Then she turned around a couple of times in a circle, and cuddled up next to the puppy, with their backs touching each other, and both fell asleep. That actually started a ritual of a friendship that lasted a lifetime. It was a win-win situation and we all got to sleep soundly that first night. From that night on, and most of the time thereafter, wherever you saw the Fluffer sleeping, you saw Harley. They drank out of the same water dish together, ate together, and literally became good buddies, and Red Dog continued to ignore them both.

Harley like all puppies was very nosey and seemed like he was always investigating anything new he discovered, yet he was a really good puppy, and not much of a chewer. He never did acquire the technique of destroying everything his puppy teeth came in contact with. However, there was one red antique chair we had that Toby's dad had given him a few years earlier, and I particularly didn't like the chair, but this was Toby's house too and he did like the chair, so it stayed. If ever a chair had a doggy dad scent on it, it was this chair. If ever a chair had to go, it was this chair!

The chair was really very ugly in my eyes. It was Victorian style and made from what looked like walnut wood and old horsehair red fabric that made me itch the first and last day I sat in it. It had skinny little arms attached to the sides made from the same walnut wood, and areas of the chair seat and arm areas were covered in the same horsehair red fabric. The seat was so worn the fabric seemed like it was getting thin from all those butts sliding in and out of it over a period of time. I had to admit it was a very sturdy and well-built chair, wood wise for its age, just very ugly. Dang, that meant there was a good possibility that it could be around forever! The only other thing it had going for it was the thing was actually comfortable. This chair actually somehow would fit anyone's butt no matter what size the butt or who sat in it. Still, it was the ugliest chair you had ever laid your eyes on, and it became exclusively Toby's chair the day it came through the doors. It also became Harley's chair the minute it was empty.

One afternoon we had to go out and we left the dogs and cat home. I was the first one to come back home and used the front door to enter the house. Now you know how it is when you walk by a room and something catches your eye because something is sort of out of place and not looking just quite right, but you just don't know what it is? I have to say it isn't always such a good feeling. I actually backed up and looked into the living room where a sleeping Harley and Fluffer were snoozing in the old red chair.

"That's funny Harley and Red Dog didn't greet me when I came in" I thought, "Are they okay?"

I stood there for a few minutes just watching Harley and the cat sleeping together in that old red chair with no sign of The Red Dog, trying to figure out what was different about the chair, and where was The Red Dog anyway? And then I spotted what it was that was different!

Harley had grown quite a bit by now and was bigger than Fluffer, but the way he was sleeping in the chair he was much lower in the seat of the chair than Fluffer was. Fluffer was actually using Harley's back as a pillow.

"Now how can that be?" I wondered, as I walked around to the other side of the chair that was facing the couch. That is when I saw how it could be.

Apparently Harley Boy had developed a chewing frenzy when we left (I am sure Fluffler put him up to it) and he actually had chewed some of the stuffing out of one side of the thin seat covering, the size of a softball. The stuffing had fallen on the floor and rolled almost under the chair, and one of the old springs had let loose and popped up through the seat some, but not quite all the way through yet. So, when the cat jumped in the chair with Harley, she was raised up more than she usually would be. Didn't bother them any; they just kept on snoozing. Red was tucked away in his cubby behind the couch ignoring me. Oh, he would peek out at me every so often, and then would back way in behind the couch as if to say "I am not taking the blame for this mess!"

"Harley" I said as he opened his little brown eyes wide. "What have you done?" Then in a flash I had quite the evil thought. "The least you could have done was to destroy it completely," I said. Together they looked up at me and both gave me a dirty look. I scooted them out of the chair, while Red continued to ignore me.

Feeling just a bit guilty, but not too guilty about wishing Harley had finished off the chair, I picked up the stuffing and tried to stick it back into the chair as best as I could. I knew I would never get that spring back in place, so I just grabbed a white lamb's wool rug I had, and an almost perfect size piece of square-shaped plywood that was left over from a project, and covered the hole in the chair. It was not the perfect camouflage, but it worked for the moment and I decided it would have to wait until Toby got home. Guess a white rug over a square-looking seat sitting in the middle of a red chair might be a dead give away that something was wrong, but time would tell.

When the doggy dad walked it the front door and headed for the kitchen, it was a precious moment indeed to watch him stop in his tracks and back up and peer into the living room where the precious eaten chair was parked. He scratched his head as he said to me half quizzingly "What happened to my chair?"

"Like the look?" I asked. "You should, as it looks better than it did when I got home. Just lift up the lambs wool rug and the piece of plywood and check it out for yourself, but I have to warn you, it won't be pretty."

Harley just sort of sat there next to me wagging his little yellow puppy tail with his rope toy on the floor in front of him, while every couple of seconds peering in at the chair as if to say "I was bored. Did I do that? Want to play now?" Red stayed behind the couch in his cubby.

I had all I could do to contain myself as Toby slowly lifted the lamb's wool, half ducking like he expected to be attacked while he slowly plucked up the now wiggling plywood balancing on the seat springs. Just as he lifted the plywood, a spring let loose and made the worst ping sound you ever heard as we both ducked, while poor Harley was literally moving all four of his little puppy legs trying to head in another direction. Red just started his maniac barking behind the couch.

"How the hell did this happen?" he said all the while he held the plywood in one hand, the lamb's wool in the other, and the two springs just a bobbing every which way. He was really pissed. "I really like this old chair" he said half-heartedly.

"Well I never did. Guess it just has to be replaced. A nice recliner chair would look and feel great right there," I said while taking my hands and making a window with my fingers. He ignored me. Harley circled around me and sat on the rug, ignoring us both. The Red Dog stayed lurking behind the couch doing nothing but taking up space now. Toby wouldn't give up, but continued to try pushing those springs back in place, and each time when they sprung with a ping they seemed like they were sitting higher. I wish you could have seen him trying to push the springs back in place while all the time muttering "Well, it isn't that bad. If I can get the springs back in place, I can live with the plywood and this lamb's wool for a bit. This can be fixed."

"Describe a bit," I said. "In terms of time is it a week, a month or years? This chair looks like hell and always did. It smells like an old dead, horse, and is really not safe now."

By now Harley had slithered back into the room, sitting next to me while occasionally looking at Toby and the chair.

"I think I can fix this, at least for now, and I have just the thing to do it with. Why there's lots of life left in that old chair" he continued to mutter while not even looking at the dog or me, then disappeared into his infamous gun room to get what he needed.

"Next time you need to do a better job," I whispered in Harley's ear as I picked him up and headed out the back door. I really did not feel like helping him fix that chair, nor did I want to be around when nothing would go right as he attempted to fix the chair. I put a leash on Harley and Red Dog actually decided to go with us as we walked by the gunroom window and announced "Taking Harley and Red for a walk, be back in a bit" and scurried so fast down that driveway I never did hear clearly what he was muttering. Whatever it was, it could not have been good.

Harley, Red, and I walked for about a half hour and when we got home we found Toby sitting in that old red chair as if nothing had ever happened, pretending he was reading one of his gun magazines. The chair did look a bit weird when he stood up, for the lamb's wool sort of just slowly rose in a square shaped pattern in the seat area. For all his sputtering and grumbling, Toby never was able to get the spring reattached just right. Yep, the chair was on its way out the door, and with

Harley's help it just might soon be gone bye bye, and a new one in its place, and just maybe a lot sooner than later. Phase one completed!

The next few days flew by, and no one even mentioned the chair, and we never heard Toby complain about how hard that seat was or even mention anything more about Harley and his chewing on it. If anyone mentioned or questioned why there was a lamb's wool on the chair, you would half-heartily hear Toby say something to the effect "I like it that way" or the other all time favorite was "Go ask Harley." The looks on the peoples' faces with his comments in reply were priceless especially when it was followed with an "Oh I see" or "Oops." Most generally if Harley was around and if he even realized they were talking about him he would simply ignore them by lying down and pretending to sleep, while Red was always hiding some place else in the house. Oh, Red could throw a few dirty looks in too for good measure; made him feel better anyway; at least I want to think it did. Then one afternoon out of the blue when we least expected it, Harley went into one of his ultimate chewing frenzies and totaled the chair. You have never seen anything so pitiful in your life.

It was my day off from work and I had lots of errands to do; so many infact, that I decided to leave the dogs at home and just go and do them and get them over with. I had taken Harley and Red for a nice long walk to tire them out before I planned on leaving thinking they would sleep most of the while I was out. For some unknown reason Harley was so full of energy, not tired like he usually was, I should have just known something was going to be amiss when one of us returned home.

Do you know how it is when you get half-way through the list of things you're doing and all of a sudden you get a premonition that something just isn't right at home, but you don't know what it is? Well, all of a sudden I got one and it wasn't a great feeling. I finished up doing what I had to do and then headed for home wondering what mess I was going to walk into when I walked through the door. I just knew what I was about to view was not going to be pretty, and it wasn't.

I pulled into the driveway and looked around slowly. The house was still standing, so that was a good thing. No one else was home so I thought that could be good or bad, or maybe even both. I walked slowly in the back door. No Harley and no Red Dog greeted me. That was a bad thing. I called to them. No dogs came. This was a very bad thing because they always met us at the door or came when we called him, unless they were up to no good. I walked through the kitchen and peered into the living room, and saw Harley and Fluffer both lying on the couch, with Fluff looking at Harley and then back at me as if to say "I'm innocent. Harley did it" look, and there it was; the scene of the crime!

I could not believe my eyes, and words cannot describe how I felt as I surveyed the mess. There sat that poor old red chair in the worst looking condition you could ever imagine. The left arm was completely torn off it and lying on the floor as if there had been some kind of tug of war game going on. The arm was so tattered and chewed I just knew there was no salvaging it. The right arm of the chair was badly mangled and chewed with all of the stuffing gone, but the wooden part was still attached to frame of the chair. The springs were no longer inside the chair seat, but on the floor in various places decorated with small pieces of worn red fabric. Stuffing was everywhere. The back of the chair was indescribable. The red fabric was so chewed and ripped to shreds, hanging off the springs that littered the floor. The right side of the chair now had a wobbling front leg. The back right leg of the chair no longer resembled a chair leg at all, but a gnarly piece of wood that one might use to start a fire. And all through my survey of Harley's work, neither he nor Fluffer moved a muscle or made any attempt to exit the room, but followed me with their eyes, occasionally looking at each other as if to say "Now we did it!" Red just stayed in his cubby behind the couch; he was the smart one this time.

Finishing up my survey of the mess, I walked over to Harley who was now sitting on the edge of the couch looking at me rather anxiously, patted him on the head and said "Good boy Harley" and then went to the kitchen to grab the broom and a trash bag to pick up the mess. Phase two completed.

At first I was going to leave the mess for Toby to see as Harley was so proud of himself, and me of him for finishing off the chair, but then I decided the special effects of the destruction created by Harley might not be as well appreciated and received as Christy's were with all of her disasters when she was younger. So I did what any good wife would do, I bagged all the stuff on the floor and placed the filled black trash bag in the middle of what was left of the chair so all could see when they too returned home for the day. We did not have to wait long!

About forty precious minutes later Toby arrived home. Unaware of Harley's decorative ability, he walked in the front door announcing he was home, and stopped dead in his tracks when he saw his chair. There he stood in shock, frozen in his tracks with his mouth opened like he was gasping for air, almost totally speechless.

"What happened to my chair?" he asked almost heartbroken.

"Harley and Fluffer must have been bored when I left to go do errands," I said. Red poked his head out from the couch for a minute then quickly backed right back in behind it again. He definitely wasn't going to get blamed for this. The Fluffler part went totally over Toby's head, or so I thought. I did not know at this point if he was going to laugh or cry, but the chair did look pretty funny, or so I thought.

Toby just stood there surveying the chair and slowly and painfully he looked inside of the trash bag as if he was saying good-bye to an old friend who had a tragic accident, pawing through the rubble with the look of disbelief on his face. Then he laughed while scratching his head.

"Well, Harley, old buddy" he said, "looks like you finally killed off my chair. Did mommy put you up to this?" he asked with a smirk on his face and hands on his hips "It had lots of mileage and I'm sure if it could talk it could tell us all some pretty good stories too. Guess we will just have to get another chair. Right mommy?"

"We could do it today if you want to. We could replace it with a nice recliner. Picture yourself watching TV, stretched out in the recliner with Harley and Fluffer in your lap and Red Dog behind it stalking everything in sight." I said. I already knew that recliners were on sale at a local furniture store ten minutes from the house, and I had been squirreling away a few bucks every week since that red chair came into the house to replace it when the time was right. Today the time was right.

Toby quickly agreed. I think down deep he was half-heartedly hoping he could get rid of the red chair and replace it with a new one without hurting his dad's feelings. I know it no longer could be comfortable to sit in. Now he could get rid of the old chair and bring home the new one and he had a legitimate excuse and story to go along with it. He seemed sad for a minute or two as he picked up the frame of the chair and brought it out to the trash area while Harley and I followed behind with trash bag in hand. Harley looked so cute as we walked out together and every now and then he would give me the look like he was saying "I did good, I did good!" That chair looked so funny sitting out there we both laughed as I rubbed my mad money I had in my front pocket. Then Toby scooped up Harley and we all got into the truck and headed to the store to pick out and purchase the new recliner.

The new recliner was a perfect purchase, and both Toby, all the cats, dogs and ferrets that have lived with us has found perfect comfort in that chair whether there is a human in it, or they just nab it for themselves.

Harley was a wonderful dog and we had fourteen years gathering many great memories and shared some wonderful adventures with him. He especially loved to go to Somerset in the mountains where we would go camping. He never had to be leashed or tied as he was so loyal and would never leave us. Oh he would run and explore the woods, but was never out of sight. He eagerly and happily accepted Sunkist, Socrates, and Patches into our home when the appeared with no jealousy or sadness. He showed and shared with them all the favorite haunts in Somerset and around the house as if to say "I'm the big brother; want to have some fun, follow me."

Sadly when he turned thirteen he started slowing down like all aging dogs and started having mini-strokes, but would recover fully within a few hours. Then one hot July day while I was at work he had what appeared to be a massive stroke, and I knew in my heart he could not recover this time. My heart was broken when my neighbor called me at work to tell me I needed to come home as soon as possible as Harley was unconscious in the kitchen with Socrates, Patches, and Sunkist laying next to him as if they were comforting him. I really think they knew he was dying. Toby was on a mission trip with our Church in Canada and would not be home for at least three more days, so he did not get to say good-by to his beloved Harley.

I hurried home and found that great yellow dog just as Ariane had described surrounded by our other dogs as if they were saying farewell to their friend, brother, and playmate. I called our vet and told her what had happened, and together Ariane and I got the almost lifeless Harley into my car and I took him to the office. Painfully the vet's diagnosis was what I suspected, and I had to make the decision to put him to sleep. I did not want him suffering and I knew Toby did not either. Later that night when Toby called home, it was so hard to tell him is faithful buddy had crossed over that Rainbow Bridge and joined our other pets that have also crossed that same bridge. I think of Harley often, especially when I am dusting off his footprint that was casted for us at the crematorium, and all the enjoyment he brought us. I hope he was just as happy with us his short time with us.

Sunkist

CHAPTER EIGHT
Sunkist Golden Boy

Harley had become very comfortable in his new surroundings by his first Christmas that year, as was Fluffer to him, and the crotchety old Red Dog had actually accepted his presence in the house too. Christmas was once again fast approaching, and on Christmas Day Toby confessed to me he had planned on buying me a yellow Lab puppy for Christmas long before I had brought Harley home. The pups he knew were due in December and were now four weeks old, and if I wanted to, we could go pick one out, but the choice was mine. The funny thing was that just a couple of days before I saw a sign that told about these pups in a local convenience store, and I had been thinking that maybe Harley needed a real playmate. Fluffer was great, but a doggy playmate would be better, because we all knew The Red Dog would never be a playmate to anyone. Fluffer would get her nose all bent out of shape for a while, but she would adjust to a new puppy. I immediately said yes and we made plans to go the next day to see the pups.

The breeder led us to a very homey environment where a lively rainbow litter of four week old Lab pups were frolicking in the fresh sweet wood shavings in the puppies' whelping bed as their mom silently supervised her babies. The momma dog sniffed us all over and wagged her tail while we looked at her babies and the breeder told us the breeding line of the puppies and their parents. We pretty much already knew the line as our oldest son already had one of theses puppies from a previous litter, now two years old from the last litter, and he was such a great dog we knew these puppies would be too.

The puppies ignored us. As we scanned the pups hoping one would discover us and come over to us, in the far corner lying upside down and wagging his little yellow puppy tail ever so fast as if to say "Here I am." Toby spotted what appeared to be the biggest puppy of the litter. This fat little puppy was the color of a lemon and very affectionate and friendly. I bent over and tickled his feet and he immediately flipped himself over and came out of hiding to me, licking my fingers and wiggling his little body all over, appearing to be happy to see a human. He looked like he had a smile on his face, and you could see the cutest, shark like puppy teeth as he smiled. I scooped him up and he just kept licking my face and fingers so gently as if to say "Take me. Take me." The other pups began to take notice there was somebody new in their room. Toby tickled his chin and belly as I cuddled him and stroked his soft fur, and I noticed his fur was even thicker and softer than it looked, and then his beautiful brown eyes gazed into mine. He just melted and cuddled even closer to me. There was no other choice in the pups; I chose him.

Toby paid the deposit, and Rick the breeder placed a little blue collar on him that stated he was mine. Because he was only four weeks old and we could not have him until he was eight weeks old, but he encouraged us to come by as often as we wanted to bond with the puppy. He needed a name other than "the puppy", so right there and then I named that little ball of wiggly yellow fur Sunkist Golden Boy because of his lemony, bright color. He was an elegant dog and deserved an elegant name. We visited Sunkist about every other day, and by the third visit, the minute he saw me, and every time thereafter he would run right up to me, still wiggling all over and wagging that tail. When he was exactly eight weeks old I took him home.

It was a snowy, crisp February evening the night Sunkist came home and Harley was stretched out in has favorite spot on the couch when Sunkist and I walked in. As usual The Red Dog was off hiding somewhere. I put my car keys on the counter and I introduced Harley to Sunkist, and Harley gave me a sarcastic look like he wanted to say "Okay so you brought this kid here and disturbed my nap, now what do you want me to do?" I ignored the look as Harley was getting pretty good at giving us "the look" now. I still think he was taking lessons from the cat. I sat next to him while holding the pup in my lap while he sniffed the puppy, and after about ten minutes of the sniffing of the puppy, he licked the pup. Harley's tail was slowly wagging as was Sunkist's, and I knew they liked each other immediately.

Harley jumped off the couch to get a closer look and stood right in front of me as he gently started washing Sunkist's eyes as Sunkist ever so gently closed he eyes and let Harley do his thing while I continued to pet them both. We knew these two guys were going to be best of buddies. Fluffer just gave me "Now what have you brought home?" look while sniffing Sunkist from the back of the couch.

As the days flew by and the puppy grew, you could tell that Harley was very happy to have a doggy playmate, and Fluffer immediately accepted him as well.. Very often you would see Harley and Sunkist outside or in the house just frockling and playing, or simply just wandering about the yard exploring or chasing some squirrel or chipmunk that happened to invade the dog's territory. The chase was always halfhearted and in fun, and neither dog made any real attempt to catch the critters that dared venture into the domain of the dogs. They were hunting dogs by breed, but I think they knew they did not have to hunt or to earn their keep, in spite of the fact that Toby was an avid year-round hunter of all game animals and was always saying in jest "Don't you think it is about time you guys start earning your keep? Do you want to go to school and learn how to become real hunting dogs?" Comments like that were always good for the eyebrows of Sunkist to raise followed by one of Harley's looks, and then both dogs would just turn their backs to him. Like they actually knew what he was talking about! The Red Dog continued to ignore both dogs. It was so amazing how long he could ignore them, but he usually gave in when he heard the car keys rattle, which meant they were going for a ride, or they all heard the doggy cookie jar rattle. Dogs can be so easy!

By the time Sunkist was nine months old he did start to show an interest in the flocks of geese and ducks that would fly over the house. He actually would jump up and follow them around the yard as they flew overhead. Since his uncle Yeller who also came from Rick Jones was an excellent duck hunting dog, and Sunkist shared the same genetic pool and was showing an interest, we started training him for hunting. Both dogs were obedience trained and loved to retrieve things, but Sunkist you could tell wanted to do more, or so we thought.

The training began and Sunkist was really doing very well with his training, and Toby thought he might be ready for his first big hunt. I knew better, but the great white hunter just would have to find out for himself. Duck and geese season was in and Toby was just itching to take the Sunkist and go hunting. The next morning Toby loaded up his boat, put his gun in the truck and Sunkist and he left for his favorite hunting pond. I just looked at Harley who was most content curled up next to my feet and said "They'll be back and I'm willing to bet it won't be pretty when they return. I bet you Sunkist won't hunt for him." Harley just gave me a look and then turned his head towards the direction of the truck as they drove away on their adventure. His ears were up, his tail was down and not wagging as his nose sniffed the air. I could tell he was disappointed he was left behind, so I put a leash on him and The Red Dog and we all headed up the road to the field where Sunkist and Harley loved to run and play. The distraction worked and within a few minutes Harley was his old self again. Of course the extra dog cookie I slipped to him might have played some part in his happiness too.

About four hours went by and Toby and Sunkist returned from their great adventure empty handed. Harley and I were on the deck just enjoying the peace while The Red Dog was under the pear tree when they pulled into the yard. Of course the two Labs were so happy to see each other; Toby was half smiling as he took his gun out of the truck while Sunkist and Harley greeted each other and Toby headed towards the house.

"How did it go I asked" noticing there weren't any ducks or geese in hand to be seen, which was just fine with me because I don't particularly care to eat either one. Everyone else does, but not me.

"Your dog has a new name Napping Hunter," Toby said rather sarcastically with a smile on his face as he continued to go inside the house.

"What do you mean Napping Hunter?" I asked very curious and a bit confused. Harley and Sunkist were now both stretched out in the sun on the deck soaking up the sun while Fluffer was over on the other side of the deck half-heartily drinking from one of the water bowls we keep outside for the dogs. Red Dog was alone as usual still lying asleep under the pear tree.

"Well, we got to the pond, I unloaded the boat, got the dog and stuff inside the boat, and headed for the cove where I like to hunt. Sunkist decided to stretch out and watch the scenery, which is okay, until I saw some geese. I called Sunkist to show him. I aimed, shot, and told Sunkist to "retrieve," but he just looked at me while raising his eyebrows and then looked at the geese in the water, and then again back at me as if to say "You want me to jump in there, get wet, and bring those things back to you? Listen Pal, you shot them, you go get them. Yourself." And then he flipped himself upside down, belly up, stretched his legs and closed his eyes with what looked like a smile on his face, ignoring me completely. And to make matters worse, there where a couple of other hunters out on there the pond who saw the whole thing happen and they both were roaring with laughter when he did all that. Their dog was working like a champ while Old Napping Hunter here just lay upside down wagging his tail with a smile on his face, completely ignoring me. It was like he planned the whole thing. I was so embarrassed for a moment or two, but I have to admit it was pretty funny. The other guys sent their dog out to get the two geese so I gave the geese to them. We all laughed and talked for a while and I told them he was your dog and probably just missed you and that is when I came up with his new name. They were humoring me as they kept saying "Yeah, right, whatever Pal."

"Good boy Sunkist" I said as I scratched the napping dog's head, "You don't have to hunt." Sunkist just flipped himself on his back, started to wag his tail faster as he looked at me in the upside down mode and a smiling smug look on his face. I could just picture a hundred and thirty pound dog in the boat doing the flip thing on his back in that boat and smiling, ignoring everyone. Sunkist frequently smiled showing his teeth if he was happy or had just pulled on trick on you. He was a great trickster and one never knew when you would become the victim of whenever or whatever he would do. And people say dogs are dumb animals.

It was Holy Thursday, the day before Good Friday when we almost lost Sunkist. We live in an old house and sometime it seems those darn recluse spiders appear out of nowhere in spite of how clean you keep your home. Sunkist was lying on the kitchen floor napping when I suddenly noticed a spider crawling up the right side of his face just below his right eye and just above his nose. I got up to remove it when I heard Sunkist yelp and he started rubbing his face with his right front paw frantically. Upon inspection I noticed the recluse spider had been squished by his right front paw, and there was a very noticeable dime size area noted on his face. This area already started to swell and he seemed like he was in pain from the bite. I immediately called our vet thinking I should give him some benedryl, but instead he told me to bring Sunkist to the office ASAP because sometimes these spider bites could prove fatal to some dogs. I put his leash on him and headed to the vet's office, putting him in the front passenger seat of the car where I could keep an eye on him. He gave me an odd look as he jumped in the car, because the dogs never rode shotgun in the front seat of the car, but only in the back seat. Half-way there I looked over at Sunkist sitting there most contently in the passenger seat, and noticed the bite area had swollen twice the size it had been ten minutes before, and the entire area was very wet looking like it was oozing fluid. Every now and then he would whimper as if he was in pain. When we finally got to the vet's office his face was swollen even more and Dr. Dillman did not waste anytime taking Sunny directly into an examination room where he gave him an injection to counter-act the spider venom. We waited there after the injection for what seemed an eternity to make sure the poor dog did not go into respiratory failure as his entire face and nose were now quite swollen.

Sunkist looked so bad because his face was so swollen and he was almost unrecognizable. His nose was twice the size it should be, as was his face. His normally beautiful brown, shinning eyes were mere slits and very dull now. In spite of all that was happening, he quietly lay next to me in his usual froggy fashioned position, with his head resting on his front paws still wagging his tail while I petted him gently. Two hours later he was discharged home with me, with the vet telling me to call him ASAP if his status deteriorated. As I drove him home I really wished Sunkist could verbally tell me how he was feeling. We all slept that night with one eye open making sure he was okay through the night.

The next morning there was basically no change in his face edema, and he seemed to be breathing his normal rate and rhythm, and his appetite was very good. I went to work and warned Toby to keep a watchful eye on him and to call the vet even if he got the slightest bit worse. At 3:15pm just as my shift was ending, Toby called me frantically and told me to meet him at the vet's office as he was headed there because the bite area on Sunkist's face had literally turned very dark and had a lot of "funny looking" drainage coming from the area. My heart sank! I knew this was not good because in humans after a bite from a recluse spider one can develop gangrene in the area, and depending what and where the area is involved it usually ends up needing surgical intervention. How much surgery could a dog tolerate in this area I wondered? How extensive had this disease process extended to and at such a rapid rate? It is not like they could amputate his face and he would survive. The negative thoughts were rampidly running through my mind, making me literally sick to my stomach. What was Toby thinking when he saw this happening? He must be worried sick too. Our animals are a part of our family and when they hurt, we hurt and we sometimes feel very helpless, as they cannot verbally tell us how they are feeling and what they really want or need.

Toby pulled into the vet office parking lot just as I did and Sunkist seemed delighted and yet surprised to see me. He did his usual body shake wagging of the tail, but not with the same gusto he usually did, and after looking at his face one could understand why.

As the day progressed the swelling of his face and head had significantly decreased, but you could now see definite signs of gangrene looking skin that had started to peek through that light yellow fur with yellowish drainage from the end of his nose to above his eyebrows. He had to be in pain as well as generally not feeling well. Toby handed me his leash and we all walked into the office not knowing what fate held for us. The look of horror on the vet tech's face said it all; it was just as bad as I thought if not worse. Toby seemed really upset, as was I when we also saw the face of the vet as she attended to Sunkist. Both of us were feeling so helpless at this point and I had this horrible feeling we could possibly be leaving there without our beloved Sunkist.

Dr. Dillman was off for the day, so Dr. Littlefield was the attending vet. She skillfully evaluated Sunkist, read and re- read Dr. Dillman's notes, asked us appropriate questions, and then told us she was going to ask the other two vets that were in the office to come in to our room and evaluate Sunkist as well. After their examinations were complete, Dr. Jones and Dr. Wolfgang could not believe what they were seeing and the time frame involved. Through the entire process Sunkist never became agitated or upset with any of them as they touched and examined him, but kept wagging his tail and every now and then would attempt to give a hand that touched him a quick, gentle slurp that indicated it was okay as they touched him, as he knew they were trying to help him.

The final diagnosis was not good; he had a very severe infection and the start of gangrene in his face and they did not feel he would survive. However, because he was only 18 months old and very healthy other-wise, we could start some IV antibiotics and see if that would help. The vets also felt we should shave the entire area on his face to see exactly what his skin was doing and maybe do some biopsies of the areas in-volved to see what else we were dealing with. We agreed to do whatever we had to do for this dog. Of course we might be forever paying for this, but we had to try treating him.

"The first thing we need to do is to tranquilize him to a nice relaxed state because the razor on his face might frighten him, and the biopsies are definitely going to hurt him" verbalized Dr. Littlefield. "And seeing how he is a big dog, we need to give him a big dose, and we might keep him overnight because of the sedation."

"You can medicate him, but I can almost guarantee he will not be calm and stay put if I leave the room as he is so devoted to me and he never leaves my side at home. I know my dog and you will not be able to get those biopsies and keep him tranquil unless I am with him. If he even suspects I am near and not next to him he will not be cooperative. He will get up and come looking look for me."

They said nothing, but they all looked at me like I was nuts. Dr. Wolfgang gave him the sedation, quietly talking to him as she medicated him while we all just watched as he appeared to drifting off to sleep. Dr. Jones had the razor getting ready to shave his face while Dr. Littlefield had the biopsy equipment ready. They all had to work fast to accomplish their mission.

Saying nothing and to prove my point, I hoped, I quietly turned to leave the room so they could do what they needed to do. Sunkist suddenly opened his eyes wide, stood up and started to follow me all the time wagging that great tail of his. The look on their faces proved to be a precious moment indeed, like they could not believe what they were seeing. I stopped and walked back to where Sunkist had been laying, and he naturally followed me back there and resumed his napping positioned. Once again without further medication he appeared to be sleeping soundly while I waited a few minutes with the vets, letting them think this time he might be sleeping. Quietly I took a few steps and he did the same thing again. "That's my boy," I thought.

"I don't believe this. I gave him enough sedation to knock out a small horse," said Dr. Wolfgang. "It's clear you know him better than we do, and he wants to be by your side."

They suggested I sit by his side on the floor to keep him calm while the procedures began. He was such a good dog. I know he was very uncomfortable, but that poor dog never moved, cried, or tried to fight, or bite any of them throughout the whole ordeal. And even though his eyes were closed the entire time, his tail just kept on wagging away Sunkist fashion, and there was an actual smile on his face as if to say "Here I am. Do what you need to so I can get better. Just don't take me from my mommy."

After everything was completed, the vets thought it might be better if just because of the anesthesia he spent the night there at the clinic.

"Did you guys not learn anything about this dog?" I asked "Do you honestly think he will stay here and be quiet, because I know for a fact he won't. You all think he is asleep right now, but the minute he thinks I am leaving he will get up just like he did before. I really think he will be better off at home with us in our environment, in his home around familiar things where he feels secure and safe. I am going to take him home. I can give him any meds he needs and I can call you if I see any changes developing. I insist on taking him home."

I just knew these vets were not buying my argument because this dog was very sick, and I knew that, but as I turned to go and get his leash from Toby who was now in the waiting room, Sunkist jumped up once again, appearing unaffected by the procedures, and started to follow me out of the room. "Good boy" I thought again and kept on walking not looking at or saying anything to them. "Guess he is going home. I'll go get his meds prepared," said Dr. Littlefield.

"If I had not seen that, I would have never believed that" said Dr. Wolfgang. "He knows what he wants and I know he is in good hands. JoAnne will bring out the meds and go over the instructions for his care with you. I know you guys realize how sick he is and he will have good care, but if you see him getting worse in any way, you call us right away. One of us will call you first thing in the morning to see how he is doing. Good luck guys and keep us posted."

"We will and thanks for being so good to him," I said. Poor Toby didn't hear a word she said. He was so focused on Sunkist's shaved face as Sunkist sat there staring into Toby's eyes as if he was trying to see his reflection in Toby's eyes. Toby, half-feeling what Sunkist was feeling said, "It looks bad Bud. You got a pretty nasty looking infection there. We gotta get you home so mommy can take care of you."

I paid the bill (thank God for Master Card) and we walked back out to the parking lot where Sunkist ferreted out my car and went to the front passenger side door immediately. Guess he was in a hurry to get out of there and get home.

"Guess he wants to go home with you mommy" Toby said. "Here, I will help you get him in."

Toby opened the door and Sunkist made one leap of faith and landed right in the middle of the passenger front seat.

"Guess he doesn't need any help" I said trying to make light of the situation. "And don't get too used to the front seat either buddy, because we all know where you are suppose to be riding don't we?"

Sunkist just sat there in the front seat looking at me like he was smiling, wagging his tail, raised his eyebrows while ever so nonchalantly while peering into the back seat, and gave me a look as if to say "Right. Back seat my butt!"

Toby started his truck and I followed him home. Sunkist closed his eyes on the way home, but I knew he was not sleeping. Every now and then he would open his eyes and look at me like he was making sure we were truly on our way home. When we did get home, Harley was so glad to see us all, and Sunkist was just tickled pink to be home again. The Red Dog was actually glad to see him too. And Harley was ever so gentle smelling Sunkist's face as he was getting out of the car. He just stood there for a minute inspecting the area and then suddenly and gently with his head resting on Sunkist's back it looked as if he was trying to say "It will be okay, Sunkist. Our humans will take care of you," then they both looked at us and headed for the back door to go inside.

Toby started to fix the dogs' suppers while I started to fix ours, but we both admitted neither of us really felt like eating. The other dogs ate just fine. We ate half-heartedly while Harley and Sunkist huddled up next to each other on the doggy bed. The Red Dog actually slithered over and cuddled with them too. We should have captured the moment on film, but neither one of us thought of it at the moment.

We went to bed early and totally worn out and exhausted. When I woke up the next morning the three dogs were still cuddled together, and sometime during the night Fluffler the cat had joined them. They all looked so cute sleeping there together, and of course you never have a camera on hand when events like this happen. And you know the moment will be lost the minute you even try to locate the camera, so you do what we all have done at some time, you savor the moment and hope you never will forget.

I got up and tried to sneak up on the sleeping animals to no avail. Their senses are so sharp. To my amazement Sunkist's face looked much dryer and no new areas had developed. There was no more swelling at all, and his eyes were much brighter. And of course his old tail was wagging.

With care and medications he had a pretty fast recovery much to everyone's amazement with no scarring or permanent damage to his fur or skin.

I cannot bear to tell the story of his death because it was so sudden, unexpected, and emotionally painful for us all. Sunkist had a pretty lively and happy life, and was always at my side, and I will never forget this wonderful fellow. Sunkist lived to be ten years old.

Patches our Bagle Boy

CHAPTER NINE
Patches

One of our neighbors was excited that the new litter of Beagle/ Basset hound puppies had arrived, and Toby just happened to be there the day they were born. Being someone who loves hound dogs, he had to go and check out the puppies on an almost daily basis, and immediately fell in love with a black and white one the day he was born. Of course he did not come right out and tell me at first what he had been doing, but I knew he was up to something when he came in the house and started rummaging through our local paper like he was looking for something. He never looked at the newspaper unless he had heard something or was looking for something. Now he was tearing the paper apart and rummaging through it, so I knew this could not be good!

"What are you looking for?" I asked

"I am looking for a cartoon with Snoopy in it. I saw a dog today and I just want to be sure of the markings. I really think I may have found a dog that looks exactly like Snoopy."

He was really excited and that verified that he was up to something.

"So, tell me where do think you saw this dog?"

"You knew that I was down to Shannon's house the day the puppies were born, and he took me out to see them. I'm telling you Judy, you have got to go down there and see these puppies. They are the cutest things. There is one there that looks exactly like Snoopy in the cartoon the more he grows; he has the same exact markings. I swear to God."

"No, I don't need to see any puppies. We have dogs enough here as is. I really think we have exactly all we can handle right here right now. Beside the vet bills are getting ridiculous. It's not cheap to bring animals to the vets any more."

"I know and I agree, but you really should see this litter of puppies."

"I'll take it under advisement and think about it."

I thought about it and decided I really did not want to go see the puppies. The weeks flew by. My gut told me he was up to something, because he was down in that barn almost every night for a while, sometimes taking the boys with him, and then one night after returning from the barn he made his announcement. I was doing some dishes at the sink when Toby and the two boys came bounding in the back door laughing and giggling.

"Pick up a bag of puppy chow this week when you get groceries will you please?"

"Why would I want to do that? We don't have any puppies" I remarked like I didn't have the faintest idea what he was up to. I was going to have some fun with this plan of his.

"Not now we don't, but I am bringing that one home that looks like Snoopy. The boys like him and I want another hound. Besides we have been calling him Patch, and he comes to that name. You are really going to like him."

"Calling him Patch? You have already named this puppy? Toby I am not trying to be mean, but we do not need another dog here. If you insist on this I will have nothing to do with him. I have enough to do as it is around here, and we do not need another dog."

"Well, you better get used to the idea because he is coming home tomorrow when the boys get out of school."

I gave him the cold shoulder the rest of the night, mainly because I wanted to continue playing the game. What he did not know was that I secretly had been going down to the barn when they were not around and I already fell in love with little guy myself. And after hanging out and getting to know this puppy, anyone could see why Toby had to have him. He was the funniest looking puppy, so funny looking that he was the cutest darn thing you ever saw. His mother was a Beagle and his daddy was a Basset hound, and he looked a little like each of them depending how you looked at him. He had a long white Basset Hound body with the long black Basset Hound ears and short little legs with windswept feet like a Basset Hound, but a fat belly that almost dragged on the floor like a Beagle, and brown and black freckles on his nose. His white face also had a black mask around his eyes, and inside that black mask his eyes looked like they had brown eyeliner completely circling both eyes. His long white body had a black patch almost in the middle like Snoopy, and a flack patch of fur at the base of his tail that sort of looked like his tail had been stuck above his butt and glued in place. His silky black ears actually dragged when he walked across the floor sniffing. He had the longest tail on a dog that I had ever seen; it was the same length as his body. Toby was right; he did indeed look exactly like Snoopy.

When Toby first brought him home I acted like I had never seen him before, and Patches almost gave it away that we had secretly been meeting when he saw me. That little devil started squirming all over and wagging his tail. The two Labs looked at him when they first saw him and then at us as if to say, "What in the hell is that thing suppose to be? What do we do with it?"

But after closer inspection of smelling, licking, and doing all the doggy things that dogs do when they see a new dog, Patch was accepted into the family immediately by the two Labs, and of course me. Of course The Red Dog kept his distance.

You could not help but fall in love with this puppy the minute you saw him. There was just something very magnetic about him. I picked him up for a closer look and to again get the smell of his puppy breath. (I absolutely love puppy breath), and Patch immediately gave me a big old slurp. He was home!

"I told you that you would love him didn't I?" said Toby.

"I hate to admit it, but I really do. He is so cute and affectionate." I still did not let on that Patches and I were old friends already as I was sitting now with Patches in my lap, holding his head and looking into that sweet puppy face of his. "But what are we going to do with you now we have you? Toby, I really think his name should be Patches because of the two patches of black fur he has on his body. You can call him Patch, but I'm calling him Patches."

"I knew mommy would love him," Paul said.

And so it came to pass that this new puppy was to have two names; Patches it was voted by me, and Patch by Toby and the boys. He didn't care what his name was as he came to us no matter what we called him. And when people would ask us what kind of a dog he was, we would say he was our little Bagle boy, (half Beagle, half Bassett) and let them figure it out. He was such a handsome dog and he sure did turn a few heads wherever we went. When he was a few weeks older, and just for the heck of it, I put a red bandana around his neck over his collar, and he actually liked it. Wearing the bandana he really did look very cool with his stature and his coloring, and before we knew it he had a very large collection of bandanas. He had every color bandana you can imagine and two for every holiday. He was so cute when we would say to him "Come Patches, I have to give you a clean bandana." He would sit right there and stretch that neck of his out so you could put the clean one on him.

Patches was also very stubborn. When he got a wild hair up his butt and he got mad at you, he would literally go outside (he could actually open the back door and let himself out) and sit under the pear tree with his back to you. He would not look at the person he was angry with until he was over his snit. You could go out and try to talk to him all you wanted to, and it was really funny watching him continue to turn his back at the one he was disturbed with. After a while he would give in and be the loving dog he usually was.

Our youngest son Paul used to take Patches a lot of places with him as a teenager, and nicked named him "My chick magnet" because every time Patches was with him, it was inevitable that some girl would come over and strike up a conversation with Paul. He met more girls that way:

"Oh he is so cute. Can I pet him?"

"Oh what a darling dog; what is his name?"

"I love his bandana."

And so on and so forth, and Paul always had a line for these girls he met through that dog, and Patches loved every minute of it too.

Now Paul had a car with a sunroof, and being young he kept that sunroof opened as much as possible. One day while he vacuumed the car, washed and waxed it, old Patches was right there sitting on the lawn taking it all in, like he was supervising the job being done. That dog did not miss a move. He loved to ride, and you could just tell he was itching to get in that car as he sensed Paul was going somewhere when he was finished with the task at hand, and he was bound and determined he was going too. Paul had other plans and Patches was not included in them.

"Sorry buddy, you can't go with me this time" he said while picking up his stuff. "I'll take you tomorrow. I promise buddy." Paul was actually carrying on a conversation with the dog as he always did and Patches knew exactly what he was saying. Patches hung his head like he had just lost his best friend he was so sad as Paul continued to pick up all his stuff and put it away.

"Paul you have hurt his feelings. Look at him. He is really sad," I said.

"He'll be okay Mom. I'll take him for a ride tomorrow, right my little chick magnet?" Paul said. "Right now I have to get ready and leave for work."

We went inside the house and left all the dogs outside, and we thought they all were going under the pear tree to lie down in the shade of the tree. At least that is where they were all heading when we walked into the house. When Paul went back outside to go to work, he said laughingly "Mom you have got to see this. Patches is sitting in the front seat of my car. He must have run down the walkway of the deck and gone in through the sun roof." We both were laughing now while old Patches just sat there patiently in the front passenger seat of the car, giving us both dirty looks like he was saying "You ain't going nowhere without me boy, so hurry up!" That dog was bound and determined he was going!

Upon further inspection we determined that is exactly what he did; he jumped on the trunk of the back of the car and leaped through the sun roof and settled himself in the front passenger seat. Dusty doggy footprints on a dark blue colored trunk of the car are usually a pretty good indicator that was plan A on the dog's part.

Now at the time we also had a three-wheeler ATV, and Toby picked Patches up one day when he was a real young puppy and set him in his lap while he rode the machine around the yard just to see what he would do. The puppy loved every minute of the ride. Toby admitted that he had created a monster, as it did not take the dog long before he recognized the engine of the three- wheeler, and because he learned to open the back door, he was outside in a flash. He would jump up in your lap or whoever was driving, put his front feet on the gas tank, and that hound would ride for hours. He really did look cute riding with those long, black ears blowing in the wind.

Patches also loved to ride in our motorboat, and actually loved the water better than the Labs did. He would get so excited whenever he saw Toby getting that boat ready for an outing. Wherever you saw Toby in that boat, you always saw Patches with his hind feet planted firmly in the front seat of the boat, and his front feet on the dash of the boat, with his long black ears blowing in the wind. Anyone else who went along for the ride had to sit in the back of the boat. The Golden Rule of the boat was the front seat was always reserved for Patches, and there were no exceptions made for anyone. And besides, like the three-wheeler, he really did look so cool with those long, black, ears and his bandana on blowing in the wind. He would ride like that for hours on end. He was a wonderful companion no matter where he was or whatever we were doing, and his sudden death left a big void in our lives. Sometime we look at the pear tree and we can almost still see Patches sitting under it with his back turned to us ignoring us. Hopefully when he crossed over that Rainbow Bridge into doggy heaven, he found a pear tree up there waiting for him to sit under.

Socrates

CHAPTER TEN
Sawed Off Socrates

Bita's babies seemed so small as she lay quietly next to them as they suckled. She was not fully asleep, but was resting after giving birth only a few hours before. The rainbow litter with the vibrant colored furs was quite the contrast to their mom's light yellow fur, and they way they squirmed about as they nursed one could tell these pups were going to be on the run all too soon. There was only one puppy that had the same color as Bita, and when I first saw him, I chose him right away to be mine. Uncle Snickers, Chris's chocolate Lab, was also napping peacefully on his doggy bed with his yellow Bunny Foofoo (one of his favorite doggy toys) tucked just under his right front foot. It was very clear how loyal he was to Bita as he was to Chris. Snickers was Bita's brother from another litter. As the two Labs were always together, it was clear he was not going to leave Bita's side for any reason, like he was saying "It's okay Bita, I'll keep an eye on your pups while you take a nap." And who knows that he didn't say that to her in doggy language?

Snickers lifted his head every so quietly as did Bita checking us out as Chris and I walked into the room to check on Bita and her pups, but both dogs resumed the semi-nap position while wagging their tails once they saw it was Chris and I there in the room with them. Snickers we knew was going to be great with these puppies because he was always so gentle and laid back with Bita when she was a puppy, and his gentleness was just one of his many characteristics.

"Well, Judy, what do you think?" asked Chris as we both had been inspecting the now sleeping pups for almost an hour. Bita had now fully awakened and she readily came over to sit between Chris and me while we both scratched behind her ears and continued to sit there watching the pups. That was a good plan on her part; she got the best from both of us and got a little break from her babies.

"I think I like that very light one next to the reddish looking puppy. Do you have any idea how many boys and how many girls there are?"

"Not yet. I thought I would wait a couple of days so she can get used to them and I want to give them a good start before we start handling them. They are so cute aren't they? The light one is yours if you want it because you are such a good friend and I know it will have a good home."

"Thank you so much, Chris. I'll have to think of a classy name for it. I'll work on that after we find out if it is a boy or a girl. I hope it is a boy because the name Socrates just popped into my head. That could be a good omen."

A couple of days later Chris called me to let me know that the pup I had chosen was indeed a male, so Socrates became his name. Now all I had to do was figure out a name for his AKC papers.

Toby was actually the one who came up with his AKC name. We were up to Chris's house playing and bonding with the puppies when Toby sort of made a wisecrack about the puppies and their sizes. You have to picture him sitting in the middle of Chris's kitchen floor surrounded by puppies, Bita, and Uncle Snickers, just all doing their doggy thing, and basically ignoring us humans.

"You know Chris, these have got to be some of the cutest and fattest Lab puppies I have ever seen. Don't you agree Judy? Look how intelligent they are at this age and how good their mom is with them. Uncle Snickers, you are really good with them too even though you are "The Big Guy' of the group and not their real doggy dad", he said while scratching Snickers under his chin. "Look at Socrates" he said picking him up and petting him. "You are just a little sawed off thing. There you go Judy" he said excited. "That can be his AKC name Sawed Off Socrates. What do you think little buddy?" he said looking right in the puppy's eyes. Socrates gave him a slurp right on his cheek.

"Works for me" I said. "What do you think, Chris?"

"Works for me too; I think that name is a winner"

"Well, I guess that is his name, but it is Socrates for short. Good job Toby" I said.

"I think it's perfect too; glad I thought of it," Toby said as he cuddled the pup.

One night after Chris and I got out of work, Toby agreed to meet me at Chris's house up the road from where we lived so we could play with the puppies. By now they had grown quite a bit and were starting to walk all over the place. They had outgrown the crate where they had been born and were now occupants of Chris's entire kitchen. Uncle Snickers as we started calling Snickers, clearly loved the puppies as Bita and all of us did. It was amazing to watch his agility walking in, around and amongst the puppies. He, like Bita would wash the pups, and would push them along gently with his great nose if the got too near the gate that kept them in the kitchen. He was even willing to share some of the doggy toys with them, but not his very special Bunny FooFoo. Every time any of the pups went towards the bunny, Snickers, fast as a sweeping bird would swoop down and grab that stuffed bunny toy while the bewildered puppies would just sit there with a look of amazement on their little faces as if to say "Where did it go? One minute is was there. Now it's gone."

By the time they were five weeks old the puppies were going outside with Bita and Snickers every day. Chris had the same underground fencing for her dogs as I did, and was comical watching Snickers rounding up the puppies, trying to keep them all within the boundaries of the fence, but somehow he managed do it.

One night after work Chris called and said she was moving the pups to an outside kennel because they were growing fast and she wanted to start weaning them away from their mom. They all were eating great on their own, and soon would be gong to new homes and she did not want Bita feeling too sad when her babies left. Chris decided to start leaving the pups in the kennel during the day while she was at work, and Toby said that he would go up and check on them during the day to make sure they all were okay. At nighttime when she got home the pups were freed so they could interact with Uncle Snickers along with their mom. One day about mid-morning when I did not have to work, Chris called to see if we would go to her house and check on the pups because the gate to the kennel did not seem to be closing right that morning before she left for work. She said she propped a make-shift gate in front of the gate, but she did not think it would keep the active puppies in place for the eight hours that she would be at work. Toby agreed to go up and see if he could fix it and I tagged along so I could play with the pups and keep them busy while he worked on the gate. Those puppies sure were glad to see us when we got there. I opened the gate to let the pups out of the kennel to give them some exercise while Toby worked on the gate. It was like a herd of horses running out the starting gates, while Bita sauntered out very happy to see Toby and me. There were puppies everywhere, and I panicked thinking that I might loose one under the porch or in the nearby the woods, so I let Snickers out of the house too, thinking they would run up to Uncle Snickers and want to play. That worked! Snickers and Bita were soon romping and playing with the pups following suit, frolicking and chasing each other. In short the chase was on! At the rate they were playing I thought they all would soon be tired and would settle right down and nap after Toby fixed the gate. I could not have been more wrong!

Forty-five minutes later all of those pups were still full of hell including my Socrates. Bita and Uncle Snickers, as Chris and I called him now, were both exhausted lying on the back steps just watching those pups play and explore. Every now and then Bita would look over at Snickers and then at me with a look on her face that could say, "What's a mother to do?" Followed by a small sigh, you could tell she was getting worn out from her pups. But, neither she nor Snickers ever lost their patience with them.

An hour later Toby announced he fixed the gate the best he could and we should round up the pups and put them back into the pen. I just had a feeling that this was not going to be as easy as it intended to be. There were puppies everywhere in the backyard and just calling to them was not the answer. I clapped my hands while calling "Here puppies, puppies, puppies." That usually worked for Chris. I knew that they would follow their mother, but I planned on putting her in the house with Snickers for a little breather from them. She was still lying on the back steps and looked like she had no intentions of going back into that kennel. So I came up with plan B.

I fixed some puppy chow as a briber to get them to all follow me back inside the kennel and left Snickers and Bita inside in the kitchen. Oh they followed me back into the kennel okay as soon as they heard the sound of the food hit against the dish, but the minute we attempted to close the gate, they stopped eating and ran through the half-closed gate like a bats out of hell. Now Toby was standing on the outside of the kennel and was supposed to close the gate as he let me out after all the puppies were inside, and he did. But what we did not expect was for the herd to stop eating and follow me back out, which they did. It took us another twenty minutes to catch those varmints, and the catching part was not easy. They had a taste of freedom and they did not want to go back into that kennel. Once again when we finally corralled them all back inside, we had to come up with a fast plan of keeping them all inside and from escaping again. While I was on the inside of the kennel entertaining them, Toby walked to the far side and called the puppies to him. The schmucks went right over to him and I made a fast exit out the gate. They soon settled down into a hog pile and fell asleep. We jumped into the truck and went home.

Socrates finally came home at the ripe old age of eight weeks and was immediately warmly accepted by Harley and Sunkist. Patches, well he was Patches. He smelled the puppy all over, gave him a quick lick as if to say "Okay kid, you taste good and so you're here. Now what?" and he then proceeded to give us the ultimate all time dirty look as if to say, "Another Lab to deal with. Oh joy!" and literally went outside and sat under the pear tree with his back to us looking into the woods that joined our property for a very long time. It was both Harley and Sunkist that literally showed the puppy around the house and the yard that first couple of days. And because he was so young, he did not have an electric collar transmitter yet, so the Labs were very protective of him. Patches kept peeking over his shoulders at him like we were not supposed to notice, but he finally gave in and had a hand in raising him too. It was only a couple of days that Patches remained in his snit mood about the new puppy's arrival. We did not expect anything else of him! Every time Socrates attempted to go out of the safe area, one of the Labs would literally herd him back where he needed to be with Patches coming up the rear as if he was reinforcing where he was suppose to stay, and Socrates went willingly. That again sort of confirms that animals are able to communicate with each other. By the second day of Socrates' arrival, Patches actually brought a toy up to Socrates, shook it in his face encouraging him to play, and they became good buddies. He figured out fast the puppy was staying, and he better make the best of it.

Socrates was such a sweet Lab. He was very intelligent, loyal, eager to learn new things, and very affectionate. He was not destructive as a puppy, but actually seemed to more interested in the dog toys and spending time with all four other dogs. He tried to be friendly with Red Dog, but quickly gave up. Socrates especially loved to lie on the couch with his head in my lap if we were watching TV or reading. Like all our pups, we trained him to a crate for safety and for nighttime sleeping. Even as he grew and aged, if he was tired or wanted alone time, you could always find him upstairs in the crate. That was his cribby, his sleeping place, his safe haven, and the other dogs respected this; not one of them ever ventured in his crate. But the cats would often crawl inside the crate with him and sleep. It was comical to see this great big dog in his crate soundly sleeping with a cat cuddled up next to him. It was so cute to see the dog awaken, often surprised to see a cat cuddled up to him, and Socrates would always very gently and quietly rise as not to disturb the cat.

One of his favorite things he liked to do was to go camping. He would get so excited if he saw us getting the camper ready, and he really loved going to Somerset where we camped frequently.

The last year of his life was odd, and when I look back there were some signs there we all did not see. By then Harley, Sunkist, Patches, and the Red Dog had all passed over the Rainbow Bridge, but we had a young Chocolate Lab named Kipper. We all think we know our pets very well, but with every animal there are signs of a chronic long-term illness we sometimes miss. It happens in humans too. Socrates would be turning nine years old in May, and he had become increasingly clingier towards us than usual, not wanting to be out of our sight. He now sighed a lot for no apparent reasons that we could see. Then in April he also started to develop an occasional dry, nonproductive cough for no apparent reason. He did not seem sick. We brought him to the vet for an examination, and everything came back normal. Still my gut was telling me there was something wrong with Socrates. Sometimes he would look in my eyes, put a paw on my lap like he was trying to tell me something was not right with him.

One afternoon in early June, he walked off the deck and softly barked like he wanted me to follow him out into the yard. He kept barking until I followed him. As we walked he would glance up at me ever so lovingly, but with a far away look in his eyes. Then he went to the area where we buried all of our ferrets and cats who have died, and he just went over to the area and lay down near one of the graves, and once again while putting his head down he softly barked. Sadly, I finally figured out what he was trying to say.

I was grief stricken. I could not believe what he was doing, but in my heart I knew. He had had all these weird, unexplainable signs for nearly three months now and no one could figure out what was going on with him.

"Socrates, are you trying to tell me you are dying?" I spoke to him as I petted him. "It is okay buddy; we love you so much and we will not let you suffer. You are such a good boy. Come on. Let's go back up to the house." I turned to go back and there sat Kipper just lying on the ground with his head on his front paws, wagging his tail very slowly, but looking very lost and forlorn. My heart was really broken now.

I knelt down to pet Kipper and Socrates came over and slipped his head through the crook of my arm, and there I sat with them both for what seemed like an eternity. You can call it divine intervention, ESP, or whatever, but I firmly realized what he was trying to tell me. I realized what was happening. Socrates did not want Kipper to be alone when he died.

I took Socrates' head in my hands, looked in his eyes and said "Don't worry Socrates; I will get a puppy so Kipper won't be alone. I promise." He just gave me a big wet kiss, leaned into me for a minute and then started back up to the deck, turned, and again softly barked like he was asking us to follow him. I had an awful time fighting back the tears that wanted to flow from my eyes.

Later on that night I told Toby what had happened out in the back-yard and how empty I was feeling.

"I know," he softly said. "I saw you out there this afternoon with the dogs and I just had a feeling too what was happening. You know actually I have been thinking all along there is something very wrong with Socrates, that everyone is missing something medically."

"I think I should start looking for another Lab puppy. Kipper is so young I don't want him to be alone." I said.

"I agree," he said.

"I'll start looking tomorrow," I said. Then we both looked down at the two dogs that were cuddled up next to each other, and Socrates' tail was slowly wagging. He seemed more peaceful and actually his eyes looked happier. We both realized right then and there how much Socrates loved us and he had gotten a message to us in the only way he knew how.

The next day as I picked up our mail, I asked in passing of our post master if he knew where there might be some Lab puppies. He said as a matter of fact he knew where there was a litter that was due and he would keep me posted. The next day there was a yellow post it note in our mail box that read:

Four blacks
Four chocolates
Two Yellows
Born 6-10-05.

"What the hell does this mean?" asked Toby as he handed me the mail. "What is it, some secret code?" he laughed.

"What is what?" I asked.

"This note I found in with the mail just now."

I read the note and started to smile.

"It is a secret code my dear. Don is telling me Bridget's pups have arrived and there are four chocolates, four blacks, and two yellows. It is all perfectly clear if you know what you are looking for" I said. Toby just smiled and said "Right!"

After a quick discussion about possibly getting a yellow puppy, I called Don who gave me the rest of the scoop on the litter. I then called Bridget and made arrangements to buy the only yellow male puppy in the litter, sight unseen, (something we had never done before) and to arrange a time when we could start bonding with him. Little did we realize that this new yellow puppy would be the best bad dog we ever would own.

Weeks flew by, we all bonded, we brought him home, and everyone adjusted just fine.

Labor Day weekend arrived and we went camping as planned with our camping friends, taking all the dogs with us. I didn't have to work that Friday before the holiday, so we decided to leave the Thursday night after I got out of work. The dogs were happy and excited as we turned down Somerset Road; even Baby Beauregard the puppy was as happy because he had been up there with us a few times throughout the summer. But something was different about Socrates that night and all day Friday. He kept wandering off alone like he was visiting old familiar haunts, like he was savoring every moment. He would come back as soon as he was called, but something was totally odd. Then that night as we were settling in for the night, it happened.

I was sitting at the table, reading our local newspaper, and Toby was filling out the log he keeps in the camper. Kipper and Baby Beau were sleeping on the bed. Socrates had been in there with them, but he came quietly out to where I was sitting, sat in front of me and put his paw on my knee. I reached down to scratch him and he did it again. He then put his head in my lap and softly kissed my hand, and collapsed, having a really bad seizure. He had never had seizures before. Though it was short-lived, it really affected him. His gait was off, he also was incontinent of urine, and drooled uncontrollably. Thankfully Kipper and Beau slept through the whole thing. We both felt helpless and terrible about what was happening. One of our friends who was also camping with us there just happened to walk in on the seizure and also could not believe what was happening. I grabbed the cell phone and tried to contact our vet who was twenty minutes from where we were camping and found out they were gone for the night. I decided I would just watch him through the night, and call the Vet in the morning if he was not improved. I gave him an aspirin, thinking if he had just had a minor stoke it would help with his circulation. Sometime in night we all fell asleep and I awoke to find Socrates curled up next to me on the couch. How he got there I will never know. I took him and the other two dogs outside, but Socrates was not doing well. He could barely walk. I went back inside the camper, fed the dogs, and watched as they ate. Socrates ate okay, but there was something that was just not right. The other two dogs sensed something was wrong too, as they cuddled near him and would not let him out of their sight.

I recalled the vet and she agreed to meet me at the clinic. Glenn helped me get Socrates into the truck while Toby agreed to stay in camp with the other two dogs while I headed down the mountain to the clinic. When we got there, Socrates had another, violent seizure event, and did not arouse very well. It was then as he laid on his side the vet and I both noticed his stomach was three times the size it should have been. When she palpated his stomach, we both could see it was his liver that was grossly enlarged, and a huge tumor could be felt. Prognosis was not good, and I remembered my promise to Socrates that I would not let him suffer. It had been a very slow growing tumor, and no one noticed it until now when it finally reared its ugly grasp. It obviously had sent out little spider tumors all through his body as he was now having seizures. His respirations were very shallow and he was semi-conscious. I made the decision with the vet's advice to put him to sleep right there and then, as there was nothing we could do to prolong his life. He did not appear to be suffering in pain at this point, and I had to keep my promise. I made arrangements to have him cremated, gathered his leash and collar and cried all the way to the campground. When I got there, all of our friends were gathered at our camper waiting for the news of Socrates. Everyone loved him and everyone was very heartbroken that I had to put him down. It was such a sad day for all of us. As we reminisced about the good times we had with him, it was Glenn who remarked that he felt Socrates knew he was dying the day we arrived. Socrates in his own way was gathering more great memories to take with him across the Rainbow Bridge.

It was the most bittersweet camping trip we have ever made, and coming home that Monday we mostly traveled in silence due to our sadness, as only a few days before we left with three dogs and now we were returning home with two. As we pulled into the driveway, Toby said, "His last days were spent where he was the happiest, and you did what was right for him. We have our memories, and we will never forget him."

I was fighting back the ears that welled up in my eyes.

We continue to camp at Somerset, but every Labor Day weekend we are there it is still bittersweet, but we will always remember Socrates and the fun and the adventures he had, and all the memories we all created together.

Kipper with Beau

CHAPTER ELEVEN
Our Kipper Dawg

While taking to Wanda on the phone one evening she told me her beautiful black Lab mix dog named Saint had been killed by a car the night before. Saint was such a wonderful dog and he was always with Wanda, and I knew she would be lonely with out him.

"Are you going to get another dog?" I asked.

"I am, but I think I want to take some time looking, and I really would like to get a Lab. I really love Sunkist and I would like to get a puppy from that line if I could."

"Wanda, I really don't know if Rick is still breeding dogs any more, but I do know where there is a litter in Williamstown and I think they are ready to go to new homes. Do you want the phone number? You don't have to buy a puppy right now, but at least it might give you an idea what's out there in our area."

While we were having this conversation little did we all know my beloved Sunkist had become sick and was dying with cancer. Two weeks later he died.

"You know maybe I will call and make an appointment to at least talk to the breeder. It can't hurt to go look at the puppies."

Wanda called the number that I gave her, and her daughter and she went to Williamstown later the next day just to look and talk to the breeder, but ended up picking out a fat little male puppy she fell in love with, and named Kipper. All puppies are cute, but Kipper was one of the cutest puppies you ever saw. He was the typical nosy puppy who was always investigating anything and everything that moved or he focused in on. Her grandson absolutely loved him. Now dogs like people all have their own personalities and mannerisms, but when I went over to see Kipper all I could think of was a miniature Sunkist as his mannerism were exactly the same. He was lying under her kitchen table chewing on one of Saint's old toys, oblivious to everything and everyone else around him at the time, just doing his puppy thing. Amazingly the only thing that was different about him was his age and his coloring. As soon as he noticed me standing there with Wanda, he quickly came over to me puppy fashion to check me out.

"Oh my gosh, Kipper. You look like and act exactly like my Sunkist," I said. "What are the odds of this, Wanda, that two dogs could be so much alike?"

Now Wanda owns and operates a wonderful Residential Care Home and the residents are all well cared for and provided for by Wanda, her husband Wayne, and staff. Animals have always been a big part in her plan of care for her residents, so when Saint died unexpectedly most of the residents missed him. Now Kipper was there, and hopefully he would liven up the place again. Weeks flew into six months, and by now my Sunkist had died, and Wanda knew how deeply I missed him. Kipper was growing into this very intelligent, loving, beautiful dog, acting more and more like Sunkist with each passing day, and he seemed to love us as much as he did Wanda. He was clearly Wanda's dog as he was always with her. But sometimes the best of intentions and plans are not meant to be, and so it came to pass some people there at the home, residents, visitors, and staff did not show Kipper much affection, and sadly some were not very nice to him. In spite of it all, he remained a very sweet and loyal puppy, and knew he was loved.

One afternoon while we were talking, Wanda seemed really sad and asked me if I wanted to take Kipper home because she knew I would give him a good home and he would be happy with the other dogs. She said she had made a decision and she wanted what was best for him. I was totally surprised.

"But you love him, Wanda. He was meant to be your dog. Can't something be worked out with that whole bunch so you can keep him? Let's give it a couple more weeks so you can think this through a bit."

"No, it can't. I have thought about this long and hard and I want him in a happy environment and for some reason people here just do not like him. He will be much happier in an environment like yours where he can play with other dogs. I know you will take good care of him."

"Are you really sure about this? This is a big decision. I know how much you love him. I will reimburse you for him."

"No, you cannot reimburse me. I told you that I have thought about this long and hard, and I want you to have him. The money is not an issue here. His well-being and happiness is more important and I know he will be happier with you guys. And besides I can always see him whenever I want to, and you can always bring him over here to visit. It is not like I will never see him again. Please take him and give him a good home."

I was still in shock by this decision, but I agreed to bring Kipper home with me.

"In that case you and Wayne will have to agree to co-own him with Toby and me, that way if something happens to us he will still be your dog. Agreed?"

"That will work. Agreed."

Wanda seemed relieved, and I gathered up Kipper and took him home. "The boys" immediately accepted him into the family" as they already knew him through playing with him at Wanda's home. He seemed right at home here the minute he came in to our house and settled right in like he had been here all of his life.

He has been such a wonderful dog and sometimes called "The good one," as he really is the good one most of the time of our current three dogs. His intelligence is amazing as is his loyalty, and he never leaves my side for very long. Oh he loves all people and will go with Toby, but the minute I appear he sticks like glue to my side. He continues to remind me more and more of my beloved Sunkist who died so many years ago. Wanda and Wayne continue to co-own him with us, and he is always very happy to see them.

Kipper Speaks:

"Well I guess you might have gotten most of the low down on me, but I must admit I am not totally perfect, but I am a handsome dude. There have been times when I have been quite naughty, well maybe not real naughty, but I have got caught in my mischievousness. I am also one of the luckiest dogs on this earth because you see I have two doggy moms and two doggy dads who love me very much, and that is a good thing. Some dogs do not even have one doggy parent who cares as much for them as these guys do for me. On my naughtiness, I must say I have been a bit devilish at times, like when I was a puppy, but not so much now that I am an adult dog. Oh I do have my moments still. Like the time Betty (a resident) left her slippers by her bed and I thought they might be a good thing to taste. You see Betty really, really loved me and was always playing with me when I was very young, and she used to take me into her room. I really liked that because she smelled good and she was fun to be with. Well anyway, this one after noon she fell asleep (she was a lot older than me) and I got bored, so I saw the slippers just sitting there, and they smelled like Betty so I decided to rest my head on them. Only I sort of started out with just nibbling a little on them, but that was so much fun I sort of got carried away and chewed them up, the heel parts anyway. Betty wasn't too mad, well maybe at first she was, then she laughed because she said they were funny looking when I got through with them. She wore them anyway and said whenever she looked at them she would always think of me. Isn't that nice?"

"Then there was the time momma Wanda put a ham in the sink to thaw out for supper and my nose was going into overload big time smelling that darn thing. Anyway, when momma Wanda went down the hall to do something I made the leap of fate and stole the ham right out of the sink and tried to take it under the table. I almost could have gotten away with it, but momma Wanda must have heard the thud noise where I dropped it, and came back down the hall. She can move as fast as Beau, and she was very upset with me, and that darn ham turned out to be wicked cold. How was I to know it was frozen? I think my tongue got frostbite. I can tell you this; I have <u>never</u> have touched anything in the sink again!"

"Then there was the time I destroyed four remote controls for the cable TV in one day. Momma Judy was very surprised the first time I did that, because I sort have learned how to open the drawer of the table where she kept it. She had to replace them three more times in one day after I even chewed up the other three. I just could not help myself. Yep, she made three more trips to the cable TV office that day to replace those remotes, and the folks there said that was an all-time record for remote replacements in one household in one day. Not a good day for her or the folks at the cable TV office, but it was fun for me while I didn't get caught. My doggy parents did outsmart me by locking the control up in the cupboard where I could not reach them. They sort of clipped my wings on that adventure. Anyway, they don't even taste good any more."

"I am the 'good one' as my doggy mom Judy calls me. We have a device called hidden fence in our yard, which is a good thing because we don't have any bugs in our fur and we get to roam about freely in our yard, well I do anyway. I especially love lying on the back deck or out in the backyard on the lawn, or sometimes in the shade under the willow trees by the backyard flowerbeds. We are not allowed out in the front yard near the road. Sometime Beau and Tracker can really give my doggy dad and doggy mom a run for it. See Beauregard makes this mad escape through the hidden fence sometimes every once in awhile with no warning that the humans can detect. Then Beau might go for months being good, and then he get this wild hair up his butt that he needs to escape from the yard for awhile, and he is like gone before you can even blink. Sometimes Tracker can figure out what he is up to and will give out the alarm baying (bark...Tracker is a Bloodhound). That rascal Beau has learned to count the signal in the hidden fence and he makes a dash for it especially sometimes when he sees his real brothers Franklin or Kona who live on our road. You see we live out in the country and sometimes we might see bunnies, or deer, or turkeys, and an occasional moose. Beau just has to play with them or just have fun chasing the bunnies and cats, and he doesn't think that about how a car might hit him and hurt him, or someone could steal him and we would never see him again. He won't chase turkeys any more though, and neither do I. He is wicked afraid of wild turkeys, me too, because a great big Tom turkey chased us in our yard one day. We were minding our business, just wandering around in the yard when a flock of them turkeys landed. We did not know what they were at first and we were very curious, so we thought we would investigate what was in our yard. That Big Tom turkey spread his wings and chased us all the way back up to the deck. Nope. We will never go near them turkeys again!"

"Anyway, getting back to Beau. He just always lives for the moment and takes off. That's my little brother Beau. He will sometimes make a run for it whenever. Not me. I am the good one and I like staying free, and I do not like that shocky thing feeling on my neck if I get too close to the magic wire that carries the shock. If I even hear those beeps, I back off fast."

"Tracker is my younger brother, and he thinks he is royalty because he is a "Bloodhound, a dog of blue blood." He forgets Beau and me are Labrador Retrievers, dogs of "pure blood" too! He may out smell us with that giant schnozzle of his, but us Labradors are the number one dogs in the country, USA that is. Ha, ha to you Tracker! Besides, I got a good smeller too!"

"I love learning new tricks. I can count rotating my front paws left, right, left. I can count to thirty, and doggy mom always says "What a good boy Kipper." I always do the one, two three shake of the paws thing for cookies. I love dog cookies, and pig ears, human cookies, and human food, but moose tracks ice cream makes me puke."

"I absolutely love going camping. I never have to be tied, because being "the good one" I stay by my doggy mom's side. I love going for rides in the car, and walks to see the horses. I especially love my buddy, Mouse who is a big dark chocolate-colored horse like me. We play ball, he nuzzles me, and he sometimes gives me horse kisses that leaves me wet all over. That's okay."

"I love my doggy toys, chasing Frisbees and balls, and stealing pears from the pear tree in the fall when they are ripe. Tracker taught us Labs how to shake the tree limb to get the pears. Before we used to just eat them when the fell off the tree onto the ground. Now we get to eat more of them. And guess what? No big poops from eating all those pears!"

"You know what I especially like to do and it is lots of fun? Every time, and I mean every time my doggy dad attempts to stretch out in the recliner to take a nap, (he calls it time spent looking at the back of his eyelids). I just wander over to our toy box and fish through everything until I resurrect an old bone to gnaw on. The noise of my teeth chewing on the bone plus the slurping of my tongue on my lips drives him nuts! He always asks,

"Kipper, must you always do that when I sit in this chair?" I just give him my cute doggy smile and carry on my mission of bugging him. He is such an easy target."

"I still think that I am one of the luckiest dogs on earth because I have my two brothers Beau and Tracker, the cats and the unconditional love of my two doggy moms and two doggy dads. That's enough about me. I could tell you stuff that would make your hair stand on end, but I won't. Read on about that Rascal Beau."

Tracker and Beauregard

CHAPTER TWELVE
General Beauregard Labrador Dawg

Bridget led us out to the barn where the three-week-old rainbow litter of ten Labrador Retriever puppies were sleeping next to their mother, unaware of our presence at first. These pups were a wonderful size for being just three weeks old and seemed very alert. So we didn't disturb or upset her while they rested. We all stood around quietly whispering and admiring each puppy. I know this sounds rather selfish, but we were hoping ours would wake up so we could hold him. You can guess we were just itching to get our hands on him. As he slept I couldn't help but notice he shared a great resemblance to our old Lab Harley that passed away a few years earlier. He had the same great head, and his yellow fur was the color of golden champagne, and his little tail was wagging ever so subtly in his sleep. Guess he was having puppy dreams already. He was really cute. They were all cute, but there was something about the little male that just stood out from the rest.

While we were looking over the puppies, Bridget's dad just happened to venture into the barn and saw the three of us in there talking and watching the puppies and their mom. Saying nothing at first he came up to where we observing, and looking over at us he solemnly said, "You folks are taking the yellow male I presume? You do realize he is the pick of the litter, and I did want him for my own? But Bridget said he was already sold and I have to accept that. I know you will take good care of him. I hear you are very good to your animals."

With that last remark he went to the far end of the barn saying nothing more, but he propped himself up on a stool where he could over look the puppies. You could tell that stool did not happen to be where it was by chance, but strategically placed there for the purpose of observing the puppies.

One by one the puppies finally awoke, wandering away from the mother and trying to find another place in the puppy hog pile that was beginning to take form as the puppies awakened. You might know ours was one of the last ones to awaken.

As he crept around looking for his mom puppy style, Bridget scooped him up ever so gently and handed him to Toby where he proceeded to try and suck the end of Toby's nose.

"So what's his name going to be?" Bridget asked.

"I don't know yet," I said. "We had to get a look at him before we decided. He sure is a fat little guy. Judging form his size at three weeks old he is going to be good size adult dog."

"His dad is good size and as you can see mom here is good size too" Bridget remarked proudly.

"Their colors are all so rich and vibrant looking," I said. "Guess we will really have to be thinking about his name, but we will let you know the next time we come over to visit him."

Toby put the puppy back with his littermates so he could nursed along with the other puppies. We stayed for a few minutes longer, gave her our deposit and departed for home. While we were driving back towards our house Toby asked me, "What was that name you said you had picked out years ago for a Bloodhound if you ever could find one?"

"General Beauregard. Why are you asking?"

"Do you really think we will ever get a Bloodhound? Be serious now. What are the odds of us finding a Bloodhound in this area?"

"You want to steal my name for the puppy don't you?" I teased.

"Well I have been thinking that that name sort of fits that puppy, but if you really don't want me to, we could name him something else I guess. I mean how hard is it to come up with a name for a dog?"

"It does have a nice sound doesn't it? Glad I thought of it all those years ago, and seeing how I probably will never find a Bloodhound, you can use the name, but it is going to cost you. Yep General Beauregard Labrador Dawg has a rather nice ring to it doesn't?" I said.

Toby had that little smirk on his face again like he had planned all along stealing my name for a Bloodhound and giving it to the new puppy. After all, he was right, the odds of me ever finding a Bloodhound in our area was a million to one shot, and beside I gave up years ago that I ever would get a Bloodhound. But, if you think for one minute that I was about to tell Toby that part of it, you can guess again. He might as well use the name; it was a good one and it seemed to fit the puppy well.

"Yes. I like that name" Toby said. "So if you agree, General Labrador Dawg, it is. He does look rather regal. We can call him Beau for short. Agreed?"

"Agreed" I said, "but you are still going to pay dearly for taking my name."

And so the puppy now had an AKC name and the house name we would call him. Not bad for a mere two hours work on Toby's part. I still do believe he plotted from the first day he knew about Beau to use that name.

So we visited Baby Beau as we started to call him three times a week, and by five weeks old the momma dog was totally exhausted from her puppies and unexpectedly stopped nursing them. The puppies were pretty well weaned anyway, and they were like little piranha, eating machines. They really were a very lively bunch to handle. Little did we know that they were a bunch of mini Marley's in progress, just a plotting and scheming once they all discovered that they had legs and mouths. One wonders if these puppies were plots from someone up above the heavens to test us all here on earth. I sure hope we pass the testings as Beau has definitely and defiantly given us a run for the money at times.

Baby Beau came home the last week in July at five weeks old. And as you guessed it, Socrates and Kipper immediately accepted him into the pack. I really had to think long and hard before taking this puppy home so young because I do not like taking any puppy from his mom before he is at least eight weeks old, and he has had a good nourishing start in his life before separating them from the litter. However, this situation was different from the normal process because the doggy mom had weaned them early due to her exhaustion. Because he was so young, I decided to set up a feeding schedule for him with supplements until we felt he was old enough to be fed like the other dogs. Beau quickly learned this schedule and we are not sure if his tummy was telling him he was hungry, he had gotten use the schedule, or he learned to tell time, but the one thing we were sure of was Beau was healthy and he was growing as he should be and wasn't the least bit proud of barking until he was fed. He soon grew out of that barking habit and I really think it was because he soon learned that there was always dry food to be found in the laundry room where we feed the dogs. You see not only are our dogs always fed twice a day with a mixture of canned food, dry food, and veggies, but there are always a couple of big dishes in the laundry room with dry food and a community dish of water 24/7 just in case they feel like nibbling or drinking. In case you are wondering why the dogs just don't gobble the food up all at once because it is there, they never have and I think it is because they are used to being fed twice a day on a routine, and they know they can eat when they need to. Humans do; we always have an access to food. Farm animals like sheep, cattle, and horses do in the fields, and so do some house cats, ferrets, and birds in cages, so it just makes sense the dogs should be able too as well. That is the way we have always done it and always will. And before you even think it, no they are not overweight, and they actually look great. They are actually smarter than humans when it comes to controlling their weight.

Franklin, Kona, and Ozzie, three of Beau's littermates also live on our road, and Beau had the good fortune to be able to play with Franklin very often during the week for a while. As I said before all of these puppies had a tendency to be like little eating machines, like piranha, eating everything and anything in sight, and it did not matter what it was that they would consume. If it even looked or smelled good to them, and being as quick as they were, the item they were zooming in on with their beady little eyeballs was gone down the old gullet in seconds. One gulp and whatever it was usually became a memory.

One afternoon when Kathy and I had Beau and Franklin out walking after a few hours of playing (they did not tire easily) Franklin very subtly and quickly gobbled a rock the size of a quarter as we walked and swallowed it. I just happened to see this out of the corner of my eye and told Kathy what had just happened. While we were distracted to see if Franklin had indeed ingested the stone, Beau quickly tried to gobble up something from the same nearby pile of dirt, but Kathy's quick eye caught him in action.

"Are you sure he swallowed it, Judy?" Kathy asked. "Beau spit out that dirt. We don't need both of you getting sick for being stupid! Why do you guys do this?"

"Oh yeah, I'm positive." I said. "Beau Spit out that stone. Can you see the dirt in Franklin's mouth and on his lips?" We were both checking out his mouth now. "He swallowed it. I am sure of it. I think we need to call the vet just in case he gets an intestinal obstruction from it. Beau stop trying to eat dirt."

"What are you guys doing to us? Do you realize how many times Franklin has done this?" Kathy said. "They are going to think we are not very responsible dog owners letting our puppies eat rocks and dirt. I better go. I'll call you later and let you know how he made out at the vets."

'Okay. Talk to you later."

Standing just beside my driveway, I headed into the house too because I wanted to double check Beau's mouth as I was sure he was harboring a rock inside of those jowls of his. Besides, I had gotten to know his little idiosyncrasies quite well in the short time since we acquired him and I was not thoroughly convinced we had gotten all the so-called dirt out of his mouth. The way he was holding his mouth I just knew he was trying to hide something. I also was feeling badly about Kathy having to make another trip to the vet with Franklin over ingesting yet another rock. Once inside the laundry room I probed Beau's mouth with my finger and sure as shooting that sneaky Beau had a rock he was chewing on hidden inside the side of his mouth. I grabbed it and threw it away. He gave me a big old sloppy kiss. I guess that must have been my reward.

Meanwhile down in North Adams it was decided that once again Franklin would be spending the night in the doggy hospital being observed overnight for the stone he decided that looked so good and had ingested. Hopefully his digestive system would kick in and he would be able to pass it successfully. Dogs! You got to love them and their living for the moment without thinking things through.

It is amazing how littermates recognize each other whether it be visual, scent, bark, or all the above if they are raised near each other. One particular afternoon I had to bring Beau to the vet for booster shots in his immunizations series. Nothing particular was different about the office that day, but when the technician brought us to the room where we waited for our turn with the vet, Beau started to perform big time. First of all he started out just sitting next to me like the good dog he could be, and then apparently bored he slid down into his famous sprawling froggy position just staring at the wall with his nose twitching like he was smelling something while we waited for our turn with the vet. Time span: 5 minutes. Then all of a sudden he slowly picked up his head as if he had been struck by lightning, and he just kept sniffing and twitching his nose in the air, but then started focusing more intently at the wall of the room he was looking at as he sniffed. Springing out of froggy position in the blink of an eye, (he always moved like greased lightening) he made one leap and he was scratching and whining like he was trying to get at something on the other side of the wall. Talk about timing, Dr. Jones walks in just as the digging of the wall commenced.

"No Beau" I said just as the vet walked in. "Sorry about that Laura, I really don't know whatever possessed him to do that."

"I do. His brother Franklin is on the other side in the next room being seen by one of the other vets. It's okay, Beauregard, we will get down to the business at hand here and then you can go see your brother." Oh the joys of living in a small community where lots of people know each other.

Unbeknowns to me before Dr. Jones walked in, Franklin was doing the very same thing on the other side of the wall of the room he was in with one of the other vets in attendance. We both finished up about the same time and as I was exiting the room to pay my bill and start for home, out comes Franklin with Kathy's daughter also leaving. Of course those two pups acted like they had not seen each other in days and started their puppy banter like they do at home. I told you they all live for the moment, and it matters not where they are. At least everyone in the waiting room and the staff had some good entertainment that afternoon.

Beau finally grew out of the babyhood thing where he needed all the feedings and the phase with the eating of rocks and chewing-everything-in-sight phase, and went straight to the "let's bark at anything that moves" phase. A little barking like barking at the knocking at the door can be acceptable, but just sitting in the yard and looking up into the sky with nothing to do except bark is not acceptable. Thank God that phase didn't last long, as his bark is a very high pitched, annoying bark that will drive you nuts after a few minutes. Then he went through the eating of the wallpaper phase. It is amazing how fast a puppy can be doing that! One minute he can appear to be napping, the next when your back is turned and you are working on the computer, while Mr. Piranha Puppy is eyeballing a loose piece of wall paper I can barely notice, and in the matter of seconds he has successfully torn and shredded a whole section off the wall and eaten it. First of all I don't want our puppy getting sick and second, the wallpaper was out of print and we didn't have enough extra to fix the mess he created. Guess that's why they invented bookcases.

Beau was completely trained to the hidden fence and obedience training began by the time he was four months old and did very well with both. Everyday we continued with his training that he seemed to have fun with. Little did we know he was plotting and scheming something that would haunt us to this day! At the golden age of eighteen months old it was like a switch went off in that head of his and all hell broke loose.

One particular afternoon Beau's other littermate brother Kona sneaked out of his yard next door and wandered over into ours, crossing via the brook that connects the yards. At least Kona has the good sense of using the brook when he wanders, and not the highway that runs in front of our houses where he could get killed. He sometimes comes over to visit, and it's no big deal because all the dogs are like kids playing, and all the dogs get along well together. However this one particular afternoon Kona got it in his head he was heading home via the road and to our surprise, Beau dashed right through the fence system with him. He never stopped when he heard the warning beeps and never yelped as he dashed through and out into the highway with Kona heading back towards Kona's house. My heart literally went right up in my throat thinking that if a tractor trailer or a car came tearing down the road like they usually do both dogs could have been killed. I was so shocked because in all the years we have had this system, we have never had any of our dogs go through it.

I grabbed one of our leashes and took off on a dead run after Beau and found him in Kona's house and brought him home. Still shaken, I checked his collar to make sure it was functioning properly and raised the frequency so he would get a sharper correction when he neared the line. That worked well all of two days when he crossed the line again. We knew the fence was intact and working because we also tested that and recently had upgraded all of the equipment and neither Socrates nor Kipper had attempted to cross the boundaries. So I jacked the setting to the highest correction on Beau's collar. That got his attention when he tried to slither out of the yard again. But he soon figured out that the brief shock he got was worth the pain as he was free to wander aimlessly about the neighborhood after he escaped again. Being a dog he just did not understand he could be killed, seriously injured, or stolen from us.

Now we were getting very worried Beau would get killed or seriously injured. Nothing was working on him and I knew it was the dog, not the system. I called the company we purchased it from, and the dealer suggested a four-prong collar set on the highest setting. That worked well for three weeks. Then he was wearing two of the four prong collars and that worked well for about six months and then he learned how to escape again.

Beau Speaks:

"I can honestly say I am one happy Lab, and I like living for the moment! My doggy dad and doggy mom never quite know what I will do next. My philosophy is keep to them guessing! Mommy is always saying, "Beau you are the best bad dog we ever had" when I do something I know I am not supposed to do. Sometimes I just cannot help myself."

"Every time the folks have tried to keep me home I have found a great way to escape. I have to give them credit, for they are persistent. But being as intelligent as I am, I have become the master of escape. It's a gift. The folks have finally figured out that I simply have learned how to count out the signals in the system. And I figured out for those brief seconds that I get zapped it is worth it because there is freedom and adventures to be made on the other side when I get to explore the neighborhood after I escape. Tracker and Kipper are no fun; they always stay home and that rat Tracker always sounds out the alarm (he bays) when I get ready to make a run for it. Tracker almost came with me once, but he backed off at the last minute. He hates that receiver collar for the fence. One day I was almost out of the yard when Patrick, mommy's nephew happened to be here visiting, and he caught me just as I was about to escape, thanks to Tracker."

"You see, mommy and Patrick were talking up near the stonewall where I usually make my exits, and mommy had her back to me, but Patrick was facing me. What I did not know was that he was watching me like a hawk. It was a trap I tell you, a trap. Just as I backed up to make my mad dash, Tracker bayed and I heard Patrick say "Beau is gong to make a run for it, Aunt Judy. Get ready."

"That Patrick can move like greased lightening, and just as I bolted he had me by my blue moose collar before I could exhale. What a shock! All that planning to escape and that skinny red-headed kid stopped me in my tracks. To make matters worse he dragged me through the fence with both the collars on and nearly fried me while Kipper and Tracker just stood there watching and wagging their tails. That was downright humiliating and that hurt my feelings. Later on I fixed that Patrick good; I went over and peed on all four of his truck tires. That's right, all four of them."

"Embarrassed and stunned, I took up sentry under the pear tree where I could see the whole yard and the humans too. I had this great plan; when I thought they were busy I would try to escape again, but I knew the timing had to be right. I waited and I tried it again and dang it, Patrick must have sneaked a big lead on me because I could barely make it to end of the driveway. Next thing I know Patrick and his friend Anthony are here putting up a big tall fence, and daddy and Andre' made a gate for the deck. To make matters worse, they moved that electric wire three feet from the new fence so if we all get too close to the new fence we still get zapped. Rats! Now I have to stay home in my yard."

"And do you know what really sucks the most? It's that darn Kipper gets to go out the gate on the deck with mommy, off his leash, no electric collar, and he gets to go all over the rest of the entire yard free. He just stays close to her like he always does because "he's the good one." I love her too, but I'm the guy who needs some space! Of course he has to rub it in when he's free as he sometimes he will walk up to the fence and look through it at us and say "Ha ha! I'm the good one. Ha ha I'm the good one. I get to go free with mommy." And doggy mom and doggy dad have no idea what he is saying; they think he is smiling and happy he is free on the outside looking in. Tracker and I just ignore him when he gets like that."

"Want to know what I do to my doggy dad when he tries to take over the recliner and thinks he is going to take a nap (closing his eyes and looking at the back of his eyelids)?I just sit, and I watch, and I wait until the timing is perfect. I wait until he gets fully reclined and looks really relaxed, and I make sure his eyes are shut. Kipper gives me the signals by gnawing on a bone from our toy box and smacking his lips. I sort of then leap into his lap, stretching the full length of the recliner with my head on his feet and my but towards his face. Oh, he occasionally will ask me "Beau don't you have something else to do other than to bug your dear old dad?" but I usually just ignore him and give him a dirty look and stretch out even further. A guy has to get comfortable you know!"

"And speaking of comfort, nighttime is the best! I get to sleep on the bed with my doggy mom and the doggy dad. Kipper sleeps next to mommy's side of the bed on the rug. I told you he doesn't like leaving her side for very long. My little brother Tracker starts out sleeping on the other doggy bed in the room, but he always sneaks up on the bed too when he thinks we are all asleep. He always cuddles up to our doggy mom."

"We get to go on vacations too, and Bob and Carole go with us. They are friends of mommy and dad. Daddy and Bob drive the truck and the camper with all our stuff in it, while us dogs ride in the car with mommy and Carole. I learned how to turn on the air conditioner in the back seat, and that drives mommy nuts in the winter. The ladies say they like it better when we go by ourselves because they can stop for coffee and pee when they want to, and we get to get out of the car and pee too. Carole always takes Kipper on the leash, and Mommy takes Tracker and me because Carole says I don't listen to her when she says, "Beau heel." She's right; I don't. She is such a pushover. But when mommy says, "Beau heel", she means it. If I don't heel, I get a correction and I really don't like it. Tracker keeps telling me it is easier to heel than get corrected. What does he know? He's a puppy yet!"

"One time we all went to Hampton Beach and it was after supper and the humans were sitting by the campfire, and Kipper and I were lying in the cool grass.(Tracker wasn't born yet) when all of a sudden I thought I smelled Barbara Sargent. I really like Barbara. She's my buddy and my doggy sitter. When we go to the beach we have to be hooked up and cannot be running free per the camp ground rules. Anyway, I jumped up and couldn't locate her, but I thought after a few minute I saw her, so I got wicked excited. I backed up and ran forward so fast because I wanted to find her that I broke my collar, and was free to run. Carole, Bob, and Mommy chased me for a long time while I was try-ing to find Barbara. People were laughing as I jumped over campfires, and I actually stole a Frisbee on my run. Mommy returned it after I got caught. Anyway I just couldn't find Barbara, Bob finally caught me while I was taking a poop. They always catch me when I do that. Any-way, Carole put a new collar back on me that mommy had while Bob held me, and mommy slapped the leash back on me. Mommy always has back-up stuff for us. After that run they all were pretty mad at me, so I knew I better heel and be good the rest of the night. We got back to our campsite and daddy wasn't too happy with me either, and then daddy put the chain on me so I couldn't escape again. I was so mad, I took a nap. When I woke up and went to stretch, they all must have thought I was planning an escape again because Bob said, "Watch him. He's got that look!" Then mommy and dad said together "Beau don't you even think about it!" Kipper gave me a real dirty look. Gee whiz. I couldn't seem to get away with nothing on the rest of that trip. So I surrendered and behaved."

"Want to know what is wicked good fun? Rummaging through the dirty clothes hamper and stealing the towels and underwear, and bringing it all downstairs and leaving the stuff all over the place. Drives the folks nuts! Daddy didn't think it was very funny one afternoon when he discovered that I had taken some of the laundry from the hamper and dragged it all outside and deposited it all on the lawn. Yep, he was just a little upset about my decorative skills. He caught me with a pair of his skivvies right in my mouth walking across the yard, and Kipper was asleep on the couch. So I guess he figured out Kipper was totally innocent that time."

"Yep, I think we have it pretty good here. All the good food and treats we get, rides in the car, a nice yard to play in, even if it is looking like Alcatraz now with the tall wire fence as a backup, and lots of toys. Best part of it is, I don't have to hunt! Guess maybe you have heard enough about me by now, so if you don't mind, I have to go take a nap and see if I can't conjure up some mischief for later."

Fifteen weeks old Tracker

CHAPTER THIRTEEN
Colonel Tracker Hound Dawg

It was a few days before Christmas 2007 and Toby's birthday, and I was upstairs just looking around on the Internet at the Bloodhound puppies. Why, I couldn't tell you. All morning as I went about my work, I kept having the thoughts of Bloodhound puppies crossing my mind for some reason unknown to me. Doesn't that just drive you nuts when stuff like that happens for no apparent reason and you cannot get something out of you mind? After a while I just went upstairs, fired up the computer while Kipper and Beau took their usual napping position next to me on the floor, and I started surfing the web on a site that my sister and a couple of other people told me about where they had successfully purchased pure bred puppies. "Can't hurt to look," I thought. By now some thirty plus years had gone by and I was resolved that I would never get the Bloodhound puppy I wanted since the 1970's. That is why Beau received the name he did, but you already know that..

Now the Internet can be a wonderful thing. I did the search thing after typing in the words BLOODHOUND PUPPIES and clicked away looking at and reviewing all the Bloodhounds that were for sale. There were no free give-a-ways for this breed; seems there never is. But, what I was amazed to see on this website were all the breeders and puppies and dogs of every age, size, descriptions, and bloodlines as well as price ranges from all over the USA, and most could be flown to our area without a problem. For some unknown reason I seemed focused mostly on the puppies. I must have viewed over seventy-five pups when I saw UNBORN in a box. I clicked on the box and saw the cutest and well-posed puppies that had been born a couple of weeks earlier. Their colors were all so rich and vibrant looking. Their eyes were so clear, and they just looked like they might be full of hell. They were definitely some of the cutest hound puppies I ever saw. A picture of the mom and daddy dog was there also, all of their descriptions, the price, as well as reviews from people who had previously purchased puppies from these people. Some of these people were as far away as England. These pups were extremely hypnotic to look at, and for some reason I kept going back to that review.

While I was looking, Toby popped into the room unannounced and asked me if I had thought about what I wanted for Christmas this year. When I told him "After all these years there was nothing I really needed, surprise me." He had no idea what I was looking at online, or that I had been looking at these puppies, but it was then that he told me he thought he would buy me the Bloodhound puppy I had wanted for all those years, and suggested we look for one online.

"Really? You're not kidding me are you? As a matter of fact I already found one." I said shocked and thrilled at the same time, turning the screen so he could also see it. "Come see how cute they are, and the price is right, and they can fly them into Albany airport."

Toby grabbed his chair and we both looked over the pups and decided to call the people. They answered on the first ring. We asked questions; they answered. They even emailed us a picture of the three boys that they did not list on their website, and finally I chose the little red one standing up in the middle. He definitely was meant to be my dog.

"So you want that one huh?" said Joe, one of the breeders.

"Yep, that's the one. He has character and looks like he is alert and very intelligent." It was very quiet on the other end of the phone, as if he was in deep thought or disbelief; I couldn't tell which. I was hoping we did not lose the connection.

Finally after clearing his throat for what seemed like forever, Joe said, "Well, he is an active little guy. Loves to play, and he always seems to be getting into mischief. Are you really sure he is the one you want?"

"He is the one. Why? Is there a problem with him?"

"No, only another guy from Texas called just a few minutes ago and was interested in him too. What do you want him for anyway?"

"Just a pet; he is my Christmas present." I went on to explain how I first fell in love with the Bloodhound breed years before, and he was the first breeder who had quality-looking dogs with an affordable price.

"Tell you what" Joe went on. "That guy never confirmed he wanted the puppy, but if you are serious, I will hold him for you. Just send me a deposit tomorrow and I will hold him until he is eight weeks old, which will be around February 12th. He still can be your Christmas present. He just needs to grow some and get bigger before we can let him go to a new home. Is that okay with you?"

"It is, and we will send the entire payment tomorrow if that is okay. Is a certified bank check or money order better?"

"It would be. Consider him yours. What is his name gong to be?"

I had no idea what I was going to call this puppy, as I had never really thought much about it, because I really had not thought about getting another dog.

"Tracker. Colonel Tracker is going to be his name." I said. For some reason that name just popped into my head. Colonel Tracker it was going to be. It was an appropriate name for a Bloodhound. Toby said after I hung up the phone we should name him Sherlock because of the investigative nature of the breed, but I knew by his little smirk he would probably sometimes call him No Shit Sherlock, (it's a guy thing), and I was not going to put up with that. I established his name was going to be Colonel Tracker Hound Dawg and wanted him to be called Tracker.

This is the first time we have ever purchased a dog without visiting the litter first and meeting the breeders face-to-face. I will admit they were wonderful to work with.

"He is just such a cool looking little dude, Toby said looking at his picture again while we were talking. Think I will call him the Tracker Dude."

And Tracker Dude is what we came to call him. His AKC paperwork is still Colonel Tracker Hound Dawg, but to all that know him he is "Tracker Dude" or "the Dude" as the neighborhood kids call him.

Weeks went by and Joe and Joyce, the breeders, kept us informed of Tracker's growth, and finally it was time to go and pick him up at the airport in Albany. It could not have been a colder day in February for a mid-southern born puppy to be transplanted in the heart of a bitter, sub-zero winter climate. Nonetheless he arrived healthy and happy with no ill effects from his air travel. His playful bay (bark) greeted us as we signed for and accepted his crate, and his playfulness at the airport was everything as described. Once in the car, he finally settled down in Toby's lap, cuddling, and smelling, and kissing us occasionally as we drove home.

Once we arrived home, I picked up the puppy while Toby carried the crate he traveled in and we went inside to meet Kipper and Beau.

They just knew the minute we arrived there was a new dog being brought into their home. I guess the crate all set up with new doggy toys for the past two weeks, just out of their reach, was the first clue. Kipper, being the oldest at six years old, I was not sure if he was going to like this new baby. After all Beau and he had it pretty darn good here as the only dogs, and now this new varmint just might infringe on their territory. The three cats sniffed, hissed and took for the high country, going upstairs into my craft room. The puppy sniffed and sniffed, and sniffed around some more while all the time Kipper and Beau were trying to figure out what the hell this thing was we brought home. It didn't smell like a Lab. It definitely was not a Lab; the ears were too long. He had long skinny legs and a tail the length of his body. Finally, Beau broke the ice by going over to the doggy toy basket, grabbing an old toy, shook it in the puppy's face, and the chase was on with Kipper coming up the rear. Tracker was accepted.

For over two hours Tracker sniffed and searched every nook and cranny of the downstairs, and discovered the cats were fun things to chase; they made the fatal mistake of coming back downstairs to check out the new dog. What the hell, if the dogs accepted him, maybe they could too. Wrong!

We have the underground hidden fence for the dogs and it is run through part of the house to keep the dogs out of certain rooms, like the pantry where I feed the cats, and our main living room. The cats know this, as they love to torment the dogs sometimes and retreat to the safe zone where dogs cannot travel. The puppy did not have an electric collar receiver on yet had and he no idea yet about the fence, so being the puppy that he was, he just chased the cats right into the room. The look of shock on the cats' faces was priceless. This was one puppy they did not want to torment, at least right now. The cats did rest easier when the pup was in training for the fence, and then they started their old mischief again. Cats, you gotta love them and their persnickety persona.

Tracker, I must say, has been a fun pup and a very intelligent pup at that. He is, however, true to his breed and can be very stubborn at times. Do you think he willingly will show the tricks he has learned when you want him to? He just sits there looking very Bloodhoundish with a look on his face that says, "Are you talking to me? You want me of royal blood doing something for a stranger? Nope don't think so!" But he loves people and very often succumbs, and very royal-like he will extend his paw to a select few to shake their hand, mostly being bribed with a cookie or something he is not supposed to eat. This I am sure he has learned from the cats.

Now I knew owning a Bloodhound was going to be lots of work as they slobber a lot, are loveable, but is also a daily adventure, and I love it! Maybe it is because we are older, but no where, no how were we prepared for a dog that is an almost constant drooling producing, spit flying, loveable, eating everything in site, high-energy dog as this Tracker is. Bloodhounds, contrary to belief, just do not just lie around most of the time and take up space, doing nothing but sleeping. They love doing just what they were bred for; sniffing and searching, and in Tracker's case getting into mischief and eating things he shouldn't. And I have never, I repeat, never in my life have I seen dog spit fly as far as it does as when a Bloodhound shakes himself. Even as an eight-week-old puppy we were amazed how much saliva these dogs produce and how far it can fly. You can read about it, but unless you experience first hand, you have no clue it can be so much.

One of the funny things that happened was when Tracker was about eleven months old. My beloved nephew Patrick had just called me up to tell me there was a special on TV about the Bloodhound breed and I should watch it. So I turned it on and was standing in the doorway of the living room watching it when Toby just happen to come in the back door with Kipper, Beau, and Tracker. The vet on TV who was giving the lecture on the Bloodhound had literally just got through saying "Folks you have never seen drool and spit fly until you own a Bloodhound. Where it all comes from is a mystery, and you have never seen spit fly with such gusto until you witness a Bloodhound shaking himself. It is totally unbelievable."

Just as she got through with that statement, all three of boys came in to greet me, Tracker stopping to shake and the big glob of spit literally flew ten feet into the air landing on the antlers of the deer Toby had mounted that it was hanging on the wall. We all know that Tracker is a great "thrower of spit", but he had really just out done himself big time. A real record it was! Kipper and Beau were as shocked as we were and both the Labs just stood there looking in amazement at this deer head on the wall, then looking back at us, and then again just looking at the glob of spit draped over the antler, waiting to see what would happen next. Tracker unaware of that he had just set a new record of a ten-foot spitting, was rummaging in the doggy toy basket looking for a toy to destroy and/or eat while we were in amazement that he had out done his old record. The next question we both had "Was the spit going to land on the sleeping cat Trouble, who was on the back of the couch, or was it going to stay there indefinitely waiting for a poor unaware visitor to sit there and have it land on him?" We waited and just kept staring, watching, watching the spit in fascination as spit does, or would it elongates, as it seemed to be just waiting for the right minute to drop and disappear? Another new record! Ten minutes had passed and the spit glob had neither moved nor stretched even a centimeter, but looked like a decoration hanging off the antler. The cat remained asleep and oblivious to what was happening. Fifteen minutes passed and nothing had happened. Another new record! Nothing was happening so I decided I better go get a paper towel and just wipe the damn thing up.

Living with a Bloodhound we have learned to have a good supply of paper towels on hand, and we are not just talking a roll or two. You never know living with this breed when the next spitting will occur, you can only be prepared! In short, if you are looking for a do nothing, lying around, looking cute, non-flatulence, (believe me they do have gas) non-drooling dog, this breed is not for you.

We love Tracker dearly, but in our early months with this dog you could never leave anything around unattended that was valuable (like my cell phone) if he was in his eating machine mode. Nothing was off limits once he made up his mind he was going to eat it or chew on it! If it even smelled good to him it was gone or chewed on. Among the things on the menu have been my Cushman Cobbler Bench coffee table, (legs and corners all chewed) three pairs of reading glasses, (Toby finally learned to pick them up if he was not using them) a cell phone, (he took in from my purse when he was rummaging for something to chew) magazines, shoes, he has even swallowed pantyhose while they were drying, a four foot piece of rope, parts of dog toys, part of a body of a kitchen witch I was making, pieces of paper towel, and a suede glove. Oh he is much better now that he is older, but every now and then when we least expect it he starts up his engines and something gets chewed. Why does he do this? Who knows? We have been trying to figure this out since he first arrived here. We do know that this dog has one heck of a digestive system, because believe it or not he has passed all the things he should not have eaten through his poop. He either has a guardian dog angel flying around him or he has really been one lucky dog because this breed of dog is very susceptible to Gastric Dilation Volvulus, sometimes called Gastric Torsion, a syndrome that could kill him. In spite of being very vigilant in keeping things out of his reach and things that could hurt him, there have been times when he has beaten us to the punch. It has been a <u>real</u> challenge trying to outwit this Bloodhound.

Now I have rambled on long enough, so I really should give Tracker a chance to speak.

Tracker age one year old

TRACKER SPEAKS:

"Did you know that us Bloodhounds are actually also called St. Hubert Hounds or Flemish Hounds? My breed actually dates back to the seventh century AD, and my name Bloodhound actually means Hooded Hound or dog of pure blood, and our facial expression is from nobility, and we are dignified. Sorry Kipper, my breed is older than yours. Ha ha."

" I am some times called "The Copper Kid" or "The Dude," and I really am very happy here with my doggy mom and doggy dad, Kipper and Beau and the cats. They are all my family. But, I could rattle on all day and half the night and you might get really bored, so maybe you might want to read one of the letters I have sent my other doggy mom Joyce and my real momma Josie. Well, actually my doggy mom Judy wrote the words for me. Read on and enjoy!"

TRACKER'S LETTER:

Hi Folks,

It has been a whole year since I came to live with my brothers the Labs, Kipper and Beau, and it has been a year of fun! Little did I know when Joyce, my first doggy mom, put me on that thing called a plane in warm Missouri I was headed to the cold winter of Vermont. That was a big trip for an eight-week-old puppy. But you know what, I really loved my new doggy mom and doggy dad and the Labs have been great too (so have the cats...they are fun to chase). My doggy mom and doggy dad really love me...I can tell. We dogs are spoiled rotten. (Yes!)

We have a toy basket full of toys, good food, treats, lots of loving, treats, rides in the car, treats, get to see friends, treats, can sleep anywhere in the house, especially the recliner, treats, get brushed every day, treats, and health care (we have pet insurance and I have my very own insurance card). I have learned lots of neat stuff too. Beau has taught me lots of things too like how to open the hamper and pull out the dirty towels and underwear and deposit them all over the house; makes for a fun thing to do when the doggy parents are out. I do not have to be in a crate any more because I grew too much and I am a whole year old now! The doggy dad just chuckled one day when I proudly walked down the stairs and into the kitchen where the folks had guests, and I had a towel and a pair of underwear in my mouth. Beau was coming up the rear barking, cheering me on saying "Great job there puppy." The guests laughed too. Samantha, Runt, and Trouble, the cats, just gave me dirty looks. They do that a lot.

I can do obedience stuff when I really want to, and when mom tells me to like "Tracker heel." "Tracker sit." "Tracker come." and "Tracker down." or "Tracker no counter surfing!" I get that last command a lot, like when I sort of put my front paws on the counter just checking to see if there is anything good I can sniff and maybe taste. I can't help it; the nose is always working! Rats! Seems like I always get caught doing that! I basically can do a lot of commands when I <u>really</u> want to, or mommy insists, and I must admit, I do have a stubborn streak sometimes. I just love to play still, just ask the Labs and the cats! I am potty trained too. I love to shake paws, especially for treats, or when I got caught chewing up dad's boots. The paw thing really did not work that all that well on the boots after I chewed them.

I have been on some fun camping trips this past summer and met some great doggy friends that camp with us. I especially like Midnight, a black Lab who is the same age as Beau, and then there is Spike a sweet Pit Bull who has a hard time jumping as high as the Labs and me because his legs are short, but he is a fun friend. I have fun with Kona and Titian, Ozzie, and Franklin who are all Beau's real brothers (litter mates) and live on our road, but they are all different colors! Kona and Ozzie are both dark brown like Kipper, who is not related to them. Titan and Franklin are jet black, and Beau is the only yellow Lab…might know he would be different. Kona and Titian live next door, Ozzie lives up the road, and Franklin lives five houses down the road. Sebastian is a honey-colored Cocker Spaniel that lives across the street and is wicked old. He tolerates me, but he is not much fun. Brutus next door is very old too and doesn't socialize much, but he is a good dog. Feruza, Brutus's mommy and my mommy take us walking on our road sometimes and that is a great adventure except we have to wear a leash when we leave the yard, and I don't like that, but I am good on the leash. I can heel you know. There are lots of nice smells on our walks.

I have learned Frisbees are wicked fast and those darn Labs all seem to always get the Frisbee first. Spike and me figured out if you wait long enough, the Labs sometimes miss, and then it is all ours, and then the chase is on!!!

I especially like Mouse, Ruby, Canelle, Bella, and all the horses that live up the road. Those guys welcomed me with open hoofs. I also have learned the bed where the doggy mom and doggy dad sleep is a wonderful thing, especially when there are no humans in it to fill it up; makes for lots of stretching room, although, I really do like cuddling up to my human mommy and dad at night. The couch and the recliner are pretty great too. I never, ever let that recliner get cold! The minute someone gets up out of it, my body is in it, except sometimes Beau beats me there first, and we have pictures to prove it. Another really neat thing I learned to do was to hide a tennis ball on Kipper and Beau. I can hide the whole ball in my mouth and still bay (bark) and Kipper and Beau cannot find the ball….it's a gift! It drives Kipper nuts when I do that because he keeps looking for the ball. But it does not work well with snowballs. Those snowballs can be cold and don't last long! I have become a pretty good pear thief. There is a video you can watch when I got caught in the act. I taught Kipper and Beau how to steal the pears too, and they are yummy and they do not make me poop!

Wayne and Linda live down the road and they really love me a whole bunch. Linda makes Kipper, Beau, and me special dog cookies that she used to make for the Bloodhound they used to have. They really love Bloodhounds, so I am special to them because they have not had a Bloodhound in a long time. Mommy told them they could visit me anytime, and I sometimes go to their house with Kipper and Beau to visit. Wayne really misses his Bloodhound and is always telling about the great adventures and fun he and Linda had with theirs. As you know my breed is not well seen in Vermont, so I must admit I do have some special friends and I really do like that a lot! I especially like mommy and daddy's State Trooper friends and they don't mind it when I get drool on their uniforms when they stop to see me. Mommy calls it Bloodhound mousse.

We have a great yard to run and play in and we have the electric underground fence, and my vet told mommy I am the first Bloodhound she ever knew that was fully trained to that kind of system. I have never left my yard. Wayne and Linda say the same thing; that they never saw a Bloodhound that was trained to underground electric fence. My Mommy is a good dog trainer and takes lots of time with us and with me when she is trying to teach the Labs and me something new. Sometimes I get bored and walk away; that is the stubbornness in me …I have an image to up hold you know.

Some people say Kipper and me are the good ones. Well, maybe Kipper really is the good one. Beau is the bad one sometimes. He used to sneak and escape our yard by running through the fence chasing a rabbit or squirrel, or his brother Kona, so Mommy used to have to tie him sometimes when he would not stay inside our boundaries, but now Beau wears two of the special collars with a special program in them, and he is now sort of good most of the time. He sometimes gets zapped when he gets too close, and he backs off. I am the really good one sometimes when I sound the alert (I bay) when I think Beau is going to make a run for it, and he gets caught every time.

Anyway guys, I am having a great time and I am definitely enjoying life and if you don't mind, I want to share some pictures and videos with you during my first year here. Some of the pictures might be blurry, because the person taking them was either laughing, or Beau was trying get in on the act…Beau is like that, yes he is. But, as mom is always saying, "Beau, you are the best bad dog we ever had."

Pictured below are dad's boots I tasted (okay, so I chewed them up). They were almost new until I got a hold of them. He wasn't too upset with me; just mad at himself since he did not pick them up before he left the house.

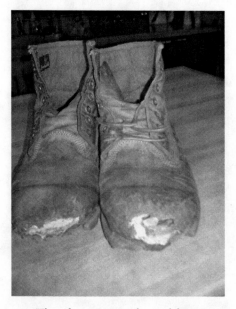

The almost new chewed boots

Below again are the same boots mommy decided to do something with. I think I could possibly have a great future designing planters.

The same recycled boots

Love,
Tracker

Sporty Beagle IV age four month old

CHAPTER FOURTEEN
Sporty Beagle IV

I almost forgot to mention anything about our last Sporty Beagle IV. Like I said earlier, throughout his lifetime Toby has had many wonderful actual hunting Beagles, but for some unknown reason they all acquired the name of Sport. Why? Who knows? Maybe it was because it was not a common name for a dog at the time, and it was the most fitting for the breed. I really think Toby just liked the name. When Sporty Beagle IV came to us it was a fluke and surprise to all of as. Someone once told me that we really do not pick out our animals, they come to us and they are part of the plan in our journey through life. As I age, I am starting to believe that.

Toby almost always hunted or fished in the mountain areas where he was as far away from civilization as he could possibly be. He once told me he really never liked society as it was today with all the hustle and bustle. He always talked about someday building a home way up in the mountains where there were no people or noise, and a person could actually hear himself think. He said he always felt he had been born a few hundred years too late. He took me many times to his favorite haunts in the mountains and I have to admit the beauty and tranquility part is absolutely correct. I also agree with him that society as we know it today has become so fast paced that we as humans for the most part have forgotten how to take time enjoy the simple and free things in life the way they were meant to be. I truly believe that our Heavenly Father has a very detailed plan for all of us on our life journey, and He places us in specific places at specific times for all of these people, events, and animals that cross our paths throughout our lives for a reason. And I truly believe how we choose e which road to walk determines our fate in our life.

Toby was hunting up around the Sucker Pond Mountain out behind the water sheds when he happened to come across an older collapsed tri-colored Beagle just laying there, totally worn out and exhausted, that had become separated from an apparent hunting party. Because of his weariness, the old dog could no longer walk or even bark, alerting a possible human in the area that he was in need of help. When the exhaustion completely took over and he collapsed, he discovered he could barely lift his head, but was able to wag his tail when he saw the human man approach. The old dog knew this meant he might finally be able to be reconnected with his master. Toby recounting the event said he could actually smell the dog before he could see him, and followed the smell to where the dog lay. Beagles are notorious for rolling in foul, rotting dead things, and because he was no exception to the breed, his actions prior to his exhaustion probably saved this dog's life.

After evaluating the foul smelling, incapacitated dog, Toby took off his cap, went to the nearby stream and scooped some water in it for the dog to drink. As the dog drank readily Toby made a fast evaluation. He knew from experience that responsible people usually had some kind of identification on their dogs' collars. Spotting the barely visible tag that was partially covered with whatever he rolled in, Toby turned the collar so he could identify who the owner of the dog was. The exhausted dog continued to drink with effort as Toby's large hands petted him while turning the collar for a better view of the tag.

"Well old boy you sure do stink, and this is your lucky day. It's a good thing I came along when I did or you might not have made it home today. Lucky for you I know your master."

Putting his now wet cap back on his head and picking up the old dog and his rifle, Toby then headed back down the mountain toward his parked truck. Resting his rifle against the truck, butt end on the ground, he carefully and gently placed the old dog on the seat, picked up his rifle, and headed for home. Once home he brought the still exhausted old dog in the house and laid him on the kitchen floor. I just happened to be coming in the back door and couldn't imagine where that foul smell was until I saw that exhausted dirty, old dog, just barley able to lift his head up laying there on the kitchen floor. The dog spotted me and started wagging his tail.

"Where did you find him?" Covering my nose I soon discovered where that rancid smell was coming from.

"Good God he stinks. Where did you find him?" I repeated, "What did he roll in?" I asked trying not to get a full whiff of him. Thank God the boys had gone fishing down in the backyard along the river that ran behind our house with their friends.

"He probably rolled in something dead up there on the mountain when he was tracking. I found him up near the water sheds, and according to the tag on his collar he belong to Asa Elwell, so you know Asa will be looking for him. He probably got on a rabbit track, and you know how Beagles can be." Toby was already picking up the phone and calling Asa.

"You mean Asa on the East Road?"

"The one and only. Seems once a year I always manage to find one of his dogs somewhere, or is it they find me? Hello Asa. Ralph Greenawalt here. Looks like I found another one of your hounds up near the water sheds a couple of hours ago, and I have him here at the house."

"That would be old Timmy. He got separated from the other two last night when we were hunting up by the water sheds, and I figured he might show up today or tomorrow. He is a wanderer you know. How does he look?"

"Well, he is pretty exhausted. I gave him some water up there and I just gave him some dry dog food and more water here at the house, and he ate okay. Right now he is sacked out on the kitchen floor, and he must have rolled in something dead because he sure does stink. Is he as old as he looks?"

"He's up there, but not that old; he sired a litter of pups not long ago, so he still has some spunk left in him. Tell you what, I will be right down to get him, and thanks for bringing another one of my dogs home. How many does this make you found?"

"Darn if I know, Asa. I lost count a long time ago. You'd do it for me if you found one of my dogs. See you in a bit."

Asa arrived within a few minutes to claim his dog and take him home. As Asa bent down to pick up old Timmy, he got a really surprised look on his face.

"Damn you stink, Timmy" Asa said, "What'd you roll in now? Dang this is the worse dog I ever had for rolling in dead stuff. Anyway old boy, I gotta get you home and get you cleaned up. A few hours rest and you should be okay. Many thanks again." Then Asa started out the front door with Timmy locked securely in his arms with Toby right behind him. Toby was going to get the doors opened on Asa's truck for him.

"You still got a beagle?" Asa asked.

"No. Ours got killed about a month ago. It was late and she went to the door and scratched to go out. Judy was right there with her and this guy who had too much to drink hit her and killed her right out. Maybe someday I'll get another one when the time is right."

"You say you can't remember how many of my dogs you have found? I do and I am so grateful to get them back. You know they are all champion Beagles and worth quite a bit of money don't you?"

"I told you I lost count a long time ago, and I know your dogs are good; good breeding and are great hunters. Like I said, I would want someone to return my dog."

"Well many thanks again" Asa said "Do you still like antique guns? Say, if you guys aren't doing anything later on stop up to the house. I have a couple of old rifles I want to show you that I picked up at a Beagle show a month ago. They are beauties. See you later then."

"Sounds like a plan. How about four o'clock?"

"That will be perfect. See you around four. Bring the boys and they can play with the animals while we visit."

"Okay. Bye Asa. See you later."

Asa drove off happy as a clam he had gotten his old Timmy back, and the feeling seemed mutual with the dog. I do declare there was a very devilish smile on that face of Asa's that went along with his twinkling brown eyes of his as he drove away.

We left to go to Asa's and arrived as planned. Asa took the boys out to see all of his dogs and I swear there had to be a dozen Beagles of different ages and puppies of every size and color you could imagine. He showed us all his dogs, and Toby recognized a few of them because at some point he had found a few of them up in the mountains. Old Timmy was looking much better having gotten a much-needed bath and brushing and more rest, but he was still pretty worn out from his nighttime adventure. He greeted us readily and seemed pretty glad to see us, but you could tell he needed rest.

Asa took us to the area where he kept all the puppies. He housed them according to age and litter once they were weaned. He led us to this one particular section where there were six very active puppies left. He opened the pen and let the boys play with them and announced that these guys were all ten weeks old and ready to go to new homes. As he was giving us all the details on these puppies, a woman came and was ready to pick up one of the pups she had reserved a week ago. Asa told the boys to just watch the puppies they were playing with, and he would be right back as soon as he completed the paperwork with her. But before he left us, we all remarked about this one tri colored Beagle that seemed friendlier and more social than the rest, and for some reason he took an immediate liking to all of us.

"That little guy seems to like you a lot," Asa said to TJ as the puppy was licking his face. "Yep he is a cutie. Right nice pup if I do say so myself. He'll make a good hunter some day. Now excuse me while I get this lady her paperwork for the pup she just bought. You kids can just continue to watch those puppies until I get back." Asa continued.

After the woman and her puppy left, Asa came back outside and rejoined us, talking more about the puppies and suddenly he changed the subject to the antique rifles. The adults went into the house to look at the guns in Asa's office while they boys continued to play with the puppies. After about an hour I announced we really needed to get home and Toby agreed. Just as we were about to go out of the door of his office, I saw Asa reach in the desk drawer and not saying a word he grab an envelope, and tucked it inside of his shirt. We said our goodbyes, and then Asa announced "Dang it, forgot something. Wait a second before you go. I'll be right back."

And with that he was off in a flash to do whatever it was he was going to do. Less than five minutes later he returned with the Beagle puppy that had taken a liking to us and handed him over to Toby.

"This is the one I thought belonged to you, but I had to make sure first. Now take him and enjoy him." Asa said with a great big grin on his face.

"But I…"

"Now just shut up and take this puppy," he said handing him over to Toby. "He is one of old Timmy's you know, so he should be a darn good hunter. I won't take no for an answer. You have returned so many of my dogs over the years, and you and your wife have always took such good care of them until I could get to your place and retrieve them, and I am ever so grateful for all you have done for my dogs over the years. Now just take him."

"Asa, thank you, but you really shouldn't do this," Toby said all flabbergasted now.

"At my age I can do any damn thing I want to, and here are his papers," he said as he reached into his shirt and handed Toby the puppy and the AKC papers. "Make sure you send in these papers now, you hear me?" Asa was smiling as he leaned on the window frame of our car.

"I will, and thanks Asa. He will have a good home," Toby said as he handed me the puppy.

"I know that otherwise you wouldn't be getting him. Thanks again and now go home before I change my mind," he said smiling.

We left not realizing what had just happened. And of course as you know his name was going to be Sport. The boys announced they thought he should be called Sporty Beagle IV, and so it came to pass that was his name.

Sporty was a very intelligent, good hunter, and very social. His hunting ability and social skills often went hand-in-hand, especially when he would get on a scent of a rabbit. Sometimes he would be gone for days. Many thanks go out to all those wonderful people who found this great dog when he would often let his nose take over his common sense, and he would take off during a hunting expedition. I am sure he is up on that Rainbow Bridge having fun just sniffing and chasing some unsuspecting rabbit that has also crossed over that Bridge, living life to the fullest while waiting for us to join them all at the end of our journey. At least I would like to thinks he is.

THE RAINBOW BRIDGE

I first discovered the poem about the <u>Rainbow Bridge</u> when our beloved Harley Davidson Dawg died, when it was placed in the gold bag along with his ashes and a cast of his great paw print from the crematorium. When I first read the poem, I cried, and I still get very teary whenever I read the poem. I have tried to find the actual author of the poem, and even though there are some theories about who the author could be, there is no actual proof because there is no copyright to be found by the actual author. Whoever first penned this wonderful poem and shared it, I want to say thank you because it offers closure to those of us who have ever loved and lost a pet, be it one or several. It is so hard to have anything we love die, and the thought that maybe when our journey on earth is over, and the possibility of maybe being reunited again with those animals that we have loved and have died before us, is more than just a romantic fantasy to some. I hope there is a Rainbow Bridge, and I hope I am met by all of my animals I have loved and lost over the years at the foot of that Rainbow Bridge when I die, even The Red Dog. And I hope that I am able to cross over that Rainbow Bridge with them all where we can make new memories and all will be together again forever.

Below is the version of the poems that accompanied Harley's ashes, and please have a tissue handy as you read; you might need it. I hope it can give comfort and closure to those who have ever loved and lost their pets.

THE RAINBOW BRIDGE

Just this side of Heaven is a place called Rainbow Bridge.
When an animal dies that has been especially close to someone
here, that pet goes to this wonderful place.
There are green meadows and grassy hills for all of our special
contacts so they can run and play together. There is plenty of
food and water and sunshine, and there our friends are warm
and comfortable. All the animals who have been ill and old are
restored to health and vigor. Those who are hurt or maimed are
made whole and strong again just as we remember them in our
dreams of days and times gone by.
The animals are happy and content, except for one small thing;
they miss someone very special to them who had to be left
behind. The animals all run and play together, but the day
comes when one of them suddenly stops and looks longingly
into the distance. His bright eyes are intent and his eager body
quivers. He begins to break away from the group as his legs
carrying him faster and faster as if he is flying over the soft,
green grass. Your pet has spotted you. And when you and your
pet finally meet again, you cling together in joyous reunion as
his happy kisses rains upon your face, and your hand caresses
his head. And you look once more into your pet's trusting and
loving eyes that have been so long gone from your eyes, but
never from your heart.
Than together you will cross the Rainbow Bow Bridge together,
and never be separated again.

Judy Greenawalt, kipper, beau, &tracker

ABOUT THE AUTHOR

Judy Greenawalt is a native Vermonter lives in North Pownal, VT with her husband, resident dogs Kipper, Beauregard, the Tracker Dude, and three cats.

　　As I grew up and even before I started school, I became fascinated with medicine and how the body is capable of healing itself for both animals and humans, and decided I wanted to be a Veterinarian. However, in the era and location where I grew up in, and even the nuns did not exactly encourage young women to go into what was considered to be "the careers of men", and neither did my parents, so second choice taken I went into the nursing field or "a career for women" instead as was suggested. As much as I have enjoyed the nursing career, over the years there has always been something missing in my life. As stated, I am a registered nurse that has quite a few other hidden talents such as dabbling in writing short stories all of my life. In college I was actually encouraged to venture in creative writing and not nursing. I also love to paint when the mood strikes me. You can often find me creating something new in the line of crafts or whatever I get an idea for something. And thanks to the wonderful technology of today, you can view some of my handiwork on my website www.kitchenwitchmaker.com if you are just a bit curious. That is just another part of "the adventures", and Toby will tell you he just never knows what I will be up to next. He always knows I'm up to something new when I ask "Would you happen to have.............?"

He always respond with "Now what are you trying to make?"

Gotta keep the adventure going you know. That is what makes life so interesting......That and dogs!

Breinigsville, PA USA
30 June 2010
240980BV00002B/4/P